10
Conversations
You Need to Have
with Yourself

Also by Shmuley Boteach

10 Conversations You Need to Have with Your Children

10
Conversations
You Need to Have
with Yourself

A POWERFUL PLAN FOR SPIRITUAL
GROWTH AND SELF-IMPROVEMENT

Rabbi Shmuley Boteach

WILEY
John Wiley & Sons, Inc.

Published by John Wiley & Sons, Inc., Hoboken, New Jersey
Published simultaneously in Canada

Limit of Liability/Disclaimer of Warranty: While the publisher and the author have used their best efforts in preparing this book, they make no representations or warranties with respect to the accuracy or completeness of the contents of this book and specifically disclaim any implied warranties of merchantability or fitness for a particular purpose. No warranty may be created or extended by sales representatives or written sales materials. The advice and strategies contained herein may not be suitable for your situation. You should consult with a professional where appropriate. Neither the publisher nor the author shall be liable for any loss of profit or any other commercial damages, including but not limited to special, incidental, consequential, or other damages.

For general information about our other products and services, please contact our Customer Care Department within the United States at (800) 762-2974, outside the United States at (317) 572-3993 or fax (317) 572-4002.

Wiley also publishes its books in a variety of electronic formats and by print-on-demand. Some content that appears in standard print versions of this book may not be available in other formats. For more information about Wiley products, visit us at www.wiley.com.

Library of Congress Cataloging-in-Publication Data:

Boteach, Shmuley.
  10 conversations you need to have with yourself : a powerful plan for spiritual growth and self-improvement / Shmuley Boteach.
      p. cm.
  Includes bibliographical references and index.
  ISBN 978-1-118-00386-2 (hardback); ISBN 978-1-118-09516-4 (ebk);
ISBN 978-1-118-09517-1 (ebk); ISBN 978-1-118-09518-8 (ebk)
  1. Self-talk. 2. Self-perception. 3. Conduct of life. 4. Communication in families. I. Title. II. Title: Ten conversations you need to have with yourself.
  BF697.5.S47B675 2011
  158.1—dc23   2011021416

Printed in the United States of America

10 9 8 7 6 5 4 3 2 1

To two great men who have walked with me through a long and challenging path:

Michael Steinhardt,
mega-philanthropist of Judaism and worthy causes globally, devoted friend, guide, and counselor, who serves as my wise inner voice, inspiring me to be a better, more devoted Jew and human being.

David Slager,
student, disciple, teacher, supporter, and friend, whose humility, dedication, and über-generosity to Jewish causes worldwide and to the teachings and work of our great Rebbe in particular, as well as to my own modest efforts, never cease to inspire or amaze.

Contents

PART III

    THE VOICE OF THE INNERMOST SELF

Acknowledgments

Iwant to first thank my former publisher and dear friend Judith Regan for helping me craft the original idea for a 10 Conversations series. The first book was *10 Conversations You Need to Have with Your Children*, which was launched on *The Oprah Winfrey Show* and continues to have a devoted following. This is probably because most of the book consists of wisdom I garnered from my wife and kids as I've tried to accomplish life's hardest and most meaningful task, raising good and decent children. True, my hair, even my beard, has begun to turn white in the process, but, boy, has it offered wisdom.

I came up with the idea for this book shortly thereafter. I have always tried to hear—or is it quash?—the murmurings of my own inner voice of conscience. Yet the book would never have been published had not Tom Miller of John Wiley & Sons endorsed the idea and helped me beat it into shape before I started writing. Tom is that unique editor with a luminous spirit whose rays you perceive on first meeting him. Unassuming, professional, authentic, and possessed of great depth, he looks for books with soulfulness that genuinely help the reader. In the process, he has made me a more focused author and a better man.

Brandon Proia did an outstanding job in helping me edit the overall book, organize my thoughts, and order them into chapters. The way I write is to first throw everything down on paper—stream-of-consciousness style—in one huge amorphous blob. Having someone like Brandon who could then take it and break it into coherent chapters so that I could then rewrite the manuscript was invaluable to an ADD guy like me. Brandon is a fine young scholar and a gentleman with a huge future ahead of him. And please don't blame me for the ADD. I wasn't like this before I had nine kids. They are the guilty parties.

Jason Kitchen has been my assistant and colleague for many years now. And his reward? His hair has now fallen out along with his teeth, and he regrets the day he was born. But for all that, he has never abandoned me, and I am grateful to him for being such a true and loyal friend and a highly developed human being.

Speaking of my kids, Mushki, Chana, Shterny, Mendy, Shaina, Rochel Leah, Yosef, Dovid Chaim, and Cheftziba—whew, let me catch my breath—thank you for interrupting me on every occasion when I tried to get some peace and quiet in order to write. Because of you, I have become a vampire, writing through most of the night and waking up with bags under my eyes like Ted Koppel. But you are all the light of my life and my greatest blessing. And you have also provided outstanding material for all of my books. So you end up helping me support you, in a weird kind of way, which I greatly appreciate.

My parents, Yoav Botach and Eleanor Paul, have given me and my brothers and sisters life and love. I witnessed my parents always try to do the righteous and moral thing, and they helped me discern the earliest sound of my own moral conscience. I am forever grateful. (I am, however, wondering where that sound has since gone.)

My siblings, Sara, Bar Kochva and his wife, Iris, Chaim, and Ateret are my best friends and are also those who gave me wedgies and beat me to a pulp when I was a child. Being the youngest can really suck. But thank you for allowing me, as a child, to discover my inner voice of self-pity.

My long-suffering wife, Debbie, is a woman of extraordinary selflessness, wisdom, beauty, and grace. She is the voice of my better self. She wants me to lead a calmer, more tranquil life in which I find contentment and satisfaction. Fair enough—but it probably ain't gonna happen. You married a man with a cavernous hole at his center. Due to your inspiration, however, I always try to fill it with good things, while consciously acknowledging that I will never be as good a person as you. How's that for an excuse? Every book I write is as much yours as it is mine. And if the book sinks like lead in the marketplace, then it's much more yours than mine.

Finally, to the Creator of heaven and earth, God Almighty, what can I say? Do I deserve all of the blessings You've given me, Lord? A wife who loves me? Nine healthy children, thank God? Enough food for all to eat? A meaningful calling that I can pursue that endows my life with purpose? I'm not sure, but probably not. Which makes it a free gift due to Your grace, Lord, for which I am forever grateful. I hope to always use Your blessings to spread Your glory and truth here on earth. May I always be worthy of Your comforting, guiding presence.

Introduction

Readers have noticed the death of conversation. Not only does the average person's vocabulary shrink year after year, severely limiting our ability to express ourselves, but we live in a culture where people do much more passive listening than active speaking. Whether it's listening to the TV, a movie, the radio, or an iPod, we absorb far more than we impart. If William Safire was correct in his argument that the telephone killed off the art of writing, then texting and e-mail killed off the telephone, in turn.

In the end, the primary culprit is the superficiality of modern culture. Real conversation is something that swells up from within. Only people who are in touch with their deepest convictions and emotions can communicate authentic thoughts and feelings to others. No wonder satisfying conversation is so rare these days.

In *10 Conversations You Need to Have with Your Children*, I attempted to inspire parents to share their deep convictions, imparting cherished values and beliefs to their children. Now in this book, the second in the series, I ask you to do something even more difficult: to know yourself, to plumb the depths of your being, and to become self-aware. I challenge you to do that rarest of things, to live an examined life. And the method you will use to achieve that goal? Simply engage in penetrating conversations with yourself.

What's that, you say? People who talk to themselves are crazy? Well, perhaps that's true—if they do so out loud, in the belief that they're actually talking to someone else. Speaking silently and sincerely to yourself, however, is a different story entirely.

If you define a crazy person as someone who lives a deluded life, then *not* talking to yourself is the surest way to lose your sanity. Those who have no self-awareness, who go through life blind to their motivations, their nature, and their soul-searing secrets—these are the people who live with fraudulent versions of themselves. They end up becoming people they never planned to be.

I meet individuals like this all of the time. One day Gary and Lisa came in for marital counseling after Gary, a successful businessman who owned a string of video stores, concluded a yearlong affair with another woman. I asked Gary, "Why did you want to have an affair?" "Easy," he said, looking at me contemptuously. "Sex. That's all. What don't you get?" "But in that case," I asked him, "couldn't you just have had sex with your wife?" "I guess I wanted sex with someone new." "Then why did you have sex with the same mistress for a full year, Gary?" At this, he was stumped.

Here was a man who had mastered his business but had gained not even a hint of self-mastery. Somewhere along the line, he ceased to know himself.

On another occasion, a married woman named Marianne came to me alone to discuss her marriage. As we talked, she revealed that she had been conducting a series of affairs. "I'm searching for something I don't have in my marriage," she said. "I deserve to be loved!"

It's true that Marianne was seeking something. But because she no longer heard the voice of her conscience, she did not know what.

Rather than engage in conversations with herself, she gave in to instinct and impulse. She began as an erotic adventurer but ended as a lonely wanderer.

Each of us is born with a unique idea of the kind of person we want to be.

This can manifest in two very different ways: visual or audial. On one hand, we see a vision of our future, of something we ought to become. On the other, we hear a voice reminding us of who we really are. A vision usually beckons from the outside, but the voice is always internal.

Usually, when people imagine their future, they see a vision of grandeur. They're the U.S. president disembarking from Air Force One, a movie star walking down the red carpet, a pop artist picking up a Grammy, a dot-com billionaire lecturing at the World Economic Forum in Davos. We've all had daydreams like these—and some of us spend the better part of our lives trying to turn them into realities. Yet we do so at our own peril, because the inner voice often gets left behind in the pursuit of our professional ambitions.

From our earliest years, that inner voice whispers to us that we were born for a different kind of greatness. As we grow up, however, we lose track of what we once heard so clearly. As with an old videocassette stored away in a drawer, if we haven't forgotten it completely, then we no longer have the right technology to play it back. Alienated from that initial vision of who we really are, we risk becoming strangers not only to others but also to ourselves.

People stripped of their inner voices frequently end up little better than psychological cripples: a man capable of seeing his appearance but not of hearing his heart; a woman who can envision a career trajectory but who is no longer attuned to her unique calling.

What does it profit a man to lose his soul
and live entirely for profit?

Many competing voices in our culture today push us to define individual success by criteria that are often alien to our true selves. Yet crying out from the depths of our being is one authentic voice that asks us to remain true to ourselves amid the noise that surrounds us.

I want you to hear that voice.

Your inner voice serves as your own personal GPS, guiding you through the byways of life. It resembles a radio station you must tune in to amid so many competing frequencies. Countless other stations clutter the airwaves and distract us by transmitting their own messages—a cultural voice, an economic voice, a religious voice. Hollywood's station tells us that life is all about glitz and glamour. The Wall Street station broadcasts that the good life is determined by the quantity of money in your bank account, rather than by the quality of your relationships. And when your own personal voice is drowned out in the ruckus of a clamoring ego, you simply go astray.

In U.S. history, one person who started listening to the wrong voice was Jefferson Davis, the president of the Confederacy. Once regarded as a great patriot, he fought and was wounded in the Mexican-American War, earning the nickname the Hero of Buena Vista. After valiantly defending the United States, he served as a senator for the state of Mississippi and even argued, for a time, against secession from the union.

Early in his life, Davis heard a calling to be forever loyal to his nation. His inner voice told him that he had to serve its ideals of liberty and freedom. But then another voice insinuated its way into his consciousness: the voice of Southern bellicosity proclaiming states' sovereignty. This new voice spoke to him so loudly that the former hero didn't realize that the principal consequences would be to prolong the evil of slavery. The outcome was tragic: a great patriot was transformed into a rebel who rose up against his own nation, simply to keep God's children in chains.

In the present day, life without an inner voice can be difficult indeed. I once counseled a man named Marty who had lost track of his conscience. He ran a successful group of restaurants until the economic downturn, when he rapidly lost almost half of his business. This man, who had once defined himself through his success, began to change overnight. He would scream at his kids and viciously unload on his wife whenever they did the slightest thing wrong. I asked Marty what was bothering him. He shook his head and said to me, "I feel like I've lost my anchor. I'm no longer tethered to any kind of mooring. I lash out at people, punish those closest to me, and I feel like I can't stop myself from abusing others."

Immediately, I knew what Marty was experiencing. His feelings of failure had completely eroded his moral foundation. His actions had no compass. He looked, acted, and felt lost. Counseling in his case meant encouraging him to listen to his inner voice of conscience, rather than seek moral direction from another person. He knew that what he was doing was wrong. He simply had to listen to himself in order to stop.

This is a sadly common phenomenon. Often when we feel lost, our first reaction is to reach out to people outside ourselves to ask for directions. Some of us, of course, don't even do that (and we all know that men are notorious for not asking for directions). Even for those who do, however, this habit of asking other people for moral direction is exactly what leads to a lifelong dependency on others to navigate the basics of our lives.

When God punished the Egyptians with the ten plagues, the second one was an epidemic of frogs. Why is that so horrible? Because the nonstop *ribbit* sound drove them to distraction. Not only that, it was deeply symbolic. The Egyptians had chosen to enslave and oppress a helpless people. They had completely stifled their own inner voice of conscience by listening to the artificial, Nietzschean voice of the will to power. Now the amphibians created even greater noise, stifling the voice of power as well.

The method of asking questions is identical to that used thousands of years ago by Socrates. He often walked around the marketplace of Athens and quizzed people about their lives. As simple as this technique was, it was so powerful that it ultimately cost him his life. The rulers of Athens didn't like the idea of people listening to their own conscience. Doing so might have made them aware that they had far fewer rights than they otherwise supposed.

Losing touch with our inner voice numbs us to life, makes us indifferent to injustice and utterly dependent on others. The rulers of Athens preferred things that way. They wanted people to rely on them for even the most basic decisions.

Contrary to the popular belief that if you talk to yourself you ought to be locked up, in truth you're *supposed* to talk to yourself—and question yourself—constantly. We are meant to have open lines of communication with what Abraham Lincoln called the better angels of our nature.

> *We need to be on the same frequency as the soul's voice, and we are meant to attune ourselves to the whisperings of something higher.*

To engage in clarifying, inspirational conversations with yourself, it's vital to understand the three healthy sources of our true inner voice.

The first source is our inspiration. You'll recognize this as the unrelenting, positive voice of motivation, lifting you up and driving you to do what's right. This is the voice that exhorts you to live for something great—and not merely "greatness" the way that our culture defines it today. If you listen to most forms of media, being rich, powerful, and famous are the only valid measures of worth. Yet true greatness comes from an inner voice that calls out, as well as from what Jews call the voice of Sinai. This voice summons us to spiritual greatness and lofty heights by telling us that we should neither squander our lives nor diminish our potential.

The second source is our conscience. This is our moral self, the part of us that wants to be decent and good at all times. To help us do the right thing, an inner voice springs forth to guide us along a more righteous path.

The third source of our inner voice is our innermost self. The song of the soul deepens our lives, awakening our spirituality and reminding us of who we wish to be. The voice of our inner spirit represents our authenticity. It identifies our unique and incontrovertible gift, the part of us that never wishes to be compromised by hearing a voice that is foreign. It is the last line of defense against the alien voice of the cultured self, which has acquired the often corrosive habits of modern culture.

Your soul's voice is your irreducible essence.

Taken together, these three sources form a symphony of personal conversation to counteract the cacophony of noise from the outside.

Your inner voice is just like your own shifting identity. You can be many things at once, to many people. Sometimes I'm a father, sometimes a husband, other times a friend. Each role is different. I, of course, don't admonish my wife as though she were a child, nor do I buddy up to my children as if they were old friends. But the same *me* resonates in each part that I play in my life. I have a moral quality, an inspirational quality, and an authentically personal quality. Without all three, I am incomplete.

Why is this so important? Because there are so many unhealthy voices vying for our attention. If we don't take control of our inner conversation, we may find ourselves listening to the wrong voice. I recently counseled a couple that had been fighting. David was a technology officer at a bank, and his wife, Linda, was a stay-at-home mom. David's job required him to travel constantly, which put a lot of pressure on Linda, who often had to care for their three children alone. To compound her stress, she also had to put up with her overbearing mother-in-law, Maria.

Tensions came to a head on Thanksgiving when Linda had to tell Maria that she couldn't come over to visit her grandkids. The children were sick, and Linda was too frazzled to receive any guests. Maria blew a gasket. Both she and Linda ended up unloading their anger on David, accusing him in separate e-mails of neglecting their needs. Imagine, the poor man was setting up a very complex international computing system for the bank, and he had his mother and his wife fighting, with him in the middle.

David and Linda asked for my help. In response, I said to Linda, "You're hearing this voice in your head that tells you to stand up for yourself. But if you were to calm down for just one minute, you'd start to hear a different voice. This voice would say, '*Now's not the time*. We can talk about my frustrations when my husband gets home—until then, I don't want to put greater pressure on him.'

"As for your mother-in-law, it may seem as if she's criticizing you, but if you put yourself in her shoes and listened to what your inner voice had to say, you would judge her less harshly. You would see that she loves her son and her grandchildren and that she's expressing that love the only way she knows how. *But your voice won't let you*— and that's because you're listening not to your true inner self, but to an ugly, defensive voice that's drowning out your authentic, inspired, and conscientious self.

"You have to hear a different voice. And the voice should say, '*Who do you want to be?* Do you want to be the kind of person who puts pressure on your husband when there's nothing he can do and he's three thousand miles away?'

"I'm not asking you to be a doormat. Be firm. And your husband should stand up for you. But start by trying to understand your mother-in-law—go see her, compliment her, learn why she is the way she is by talking to her. The reason you're upset is not because your mother-in-law is a threat to you, nor is it because your husband doesn't stand up for you. The reason you're upset is that you *know* you're not being true to yourself. And it's all because you're not listening to your inner voice."

There are far more dangerous voices out there as well. If a designer can implant a voice inside your head that tells you you're not pretty enough, you'll spend all of your money on expensive clothing. If an author can get you to see your own obesity whenever you look in the mirror, then you'll buy his diet book. And if a candidate for office can get you to hear his voice about the nation's tax revenues going down the toilet with out-of-control spending, then he can convince you to pull the lever for him in the voting booth. Yet in each of these cases, you have heard an external voice that did not inspire but instead made you feel bad about yourself.

On my TV show, *Shalom in the Home*, I worked with a seventeen-year-old girl from New Jersey who was battling life-threatening anorexia. She weighed less than a hundred pounds, yet she continued to starve herself. She told me that she listened to an inner voice she called "Ed," for eating disorder. She thought the voice was her friend. It took me many days to convince her that Ed was no pal but rather her assailant and potential killer.

To facilitate that awareness, my producers and I decided to conduct an experiment. They dressed me up with a stocking over my face so that I looked like a guy who robs a liquor store. I walked into her living room like that, and she asked me what I was supposed to be. In a low baritone, I told her that I was Ed. I spoke softly, telling her that her figure and facial features could always be improved on. I told her she was becoming heavier and less attractive every time she ate. She began to associate the voice with my frightening appearance. She realized that Ed was not her voice but rather an outside voice produced by a culture that reduces women to a collection of stick-thin body parts.

Each of us has an Ed whom we listen to, and we're susceptible to his negativity for many reasons. Foremost among them is the absence of adequate love in our childhood. Our lives are so busy, our parents so harassed, that something is bound to give. It's usually quality time with family that suffers. I don't think any of us are being given the nurturing love we really need in order to feel adequate. As we strive to make up for the deficiency, we lead lives that are so frenetic, we never have time to hear ourselves think.

I want you to ignore negative inner conversations such as these. To counter them, listen to your voice of conscience, of inspiration, and of self. The true inner voice, your own voice that serves as the bulwark against all external forces, comes directly from these three sources.

This book is my prayer that we hear our inner voice and heed what it has to say.

In a conversation with ourselves, content is all-important. It's not enough to talk to ourselves to no purpose—what we say matters. The pep talks we give ourselves will determine the people we become. If we have wrong conversations with ourselves, we risk becoming people we don't want to be.

In this book, I've assembled the ten most important conversations you can have with yourself and included a few exercises, or self-talks, in each chapter. You can use them to reshape your character; drown out the voices of self-defense, resentment, and jealousy; and inspire yourself with what your soul has to say. I've divided these ten conversations into three groups based on the corresponding inner voices you must consult: inspiration, conscience, and inner self.

First, you will speak to yourself with the voice of inspiration, which motivates you to be a greater person than you ever believed possible. With this voice, you will learn to embrace hunger, choose love over attention, use your ego and ambition, and defy our society's culture of death.

Next, you will learn to speak with your voice of conscience, choosing to do what is right over what comes easiest. You will comprehend how to "do your way to feeling," see yourself in the third person (to obtain a truer picture of yourself), and live as a blessing, rather than as a burden.

In the end, you will speak with the deepest voice of all, the voice of your inner self—channeling the essence of who you really are. With this voice you will remind yourself of the importance of struggle, of always asking, and of knowing your own individual gift, above all.

These ten conversations and the voices they spring from speak to our character on the deepest level. At the end of each chapter I've also listed questions you can ask yourself, to spur further self-talk.

When answering them, use them as a guide for future action and development. These conversations aren't supposed to be a script you read from. Only by looking deep within and locating your truest inner voices can you move forward and live a better life.

For the sake of brevity, I refer to these conversations by the term *self-talk* throughout the book. The self-talks that you have will help you develop a voice uniquely informed by morality, inspiration, and your own innermost authenticity.

Now is the time. Knock-knock. It's your conscience. Listen to what it has to say.

PART I

The Voice of Inspiration

I

Embrace Hunger

I will inspire myself to never be satisfied with
superficiality and always hunger for depth.

Everything in today's culture seems designed to satisfy some urge
or whim. After all, Americans are called *consumers* for a reason.
For us, consumption has become a religion, indulgence a new god.
Yet how strange that half of the population seems prepared to squander everything important in the pursuit of material success, while the
rest are content to gorge themselves on junk food in front of reality
television. At issue is the most basic urge of all: hunger.

Simply stated, Americans will do anything to avoid being hungry. We hunger in order to eat. We hunger in order to become sati-
ated. We focus on feeding our lesser desires. Yet we reject hunger as
a state of being.

As a result, we lose our appetite for more important things. We
spend our money on ephemeral objects that bring us instant but not

lasting joy. We squander so much of our valuable time on activities such as television and Internet browsing that serve no real higher purpose. We are rarely content in our larger lives, but rather than address our discontent we simply stuff ourselves full of junk that temporarily masks our deeper cravings.

Dennis was married to Shirley for eleven years. They lived in Toronto, but Dennis spent the weekdays in Montreal, where he ran his own business. One day Dennis's secretary came into the office with a black eye. Her husband had hit her. Dennis sprang into res-cuer mode, counseling the woman, persuading her to break up with her husband, and helping her move into a new apartment with her kids. It wasn't long before Dennis and his secretary developed deep feelings for each other. An affair ensued, and Dennis was living a double life with a new family in Montreal.

When Shirley found out, she went ballistic. After calming her down, I said to Dennis, "There is no merit in saving one family while destroying another. You chose to rescue a woman while hurting your wife. You have to cut off the relationship." He said me, "But I care about her. I can't just get rid of her."

Then I had to explain to him, "I'm sorry, Dennis, but you just don't know yourself. You lost your hunger to be a hero to your own family and to achieve one of the greatest accomplishments a man is capable of, namely, to raise a stable and loving family after emerging from an unstable and broken one. Instead, you decided to play the great Hollywood hero who rescues a damsel in distress. You lost your deeper, lifelong desire to have a positive effect with your life, and in the process, you created deep pain for two families."

Dennis took my words to heart. He told his secretary he was sorry for the mistakes he had made but that he could no longer stay in touch with her. He paid a few months of her rent and cut himself off from her. As of this writing, he and his wife, who has forgiven him, are still struggling to save their marriage.

Our culture may tell you to indulge and satisfy your cravings, but I have a very different message: *we all need to embrace hunger.* Not every attraction a man or woman has is meant to be indulged, and not every item we see on sale at the department store is meant to be bought.

Admit the truth to yourself sincerely and seriously in deep self-talk. Consult your inner voice of inspiration, which motivates you to be more than you are and calls you to greater things. Then speak aloud,

I'm looking at my life, and I'm wondering why I find it so difficult to be disciplined. I'm not at the weight I want to be. I live outside my means. My kids' lives are passing me by, and I'm too busy watching TV to pay attention. I love my spouse, but we could be a lot closer. We don't speak as much as we used to. Our conversations are about all of the practical stuff and never about romance. In fact, the practical things seem to be taking over my life completely.

I have to stop rushing to fill every need. I have to recognize that desire is the essential engine of my life, and by immediately satiating every need, I not only expend my precious resources, but I also lose the capacity to want.

I have to learn to embrace hunger.

Hunger is so much a part of our everyday lives. To seek out its roots, we must return to the first and most profound story of the Bible.

In Eden, Adam and Eve live in a beautiful garden. They have youth and health, and, best of all, they have each other. But then, in a climactic moment, everything changes.

A serpent approaches Eve and tantalizes her with a morsel of fruit she is not permitted to eat. If she would only take a bite, it hisses, the fruit would bestow on her knowledge she never knew she lacked, satisfying desires she never guessed she had. Tragically, Eve takes the bait.

So, what is this fruit (so often presented as an apple, although it was probably a fig)? It symbolizes all of the pleasures in life that are outside our reach: the dress we can't afford, the vacation that is too expensive for our family budget, the woman whom you're not married to who is off-limits. Yet it's more than that. It also represents the mistake of trying to live other people's lives. It's the envy you feel when watching *Entertainment Tonight*. It's the voice of jealousy that whispers to you when you read *People* magazine and see the house where Lady Gaga lives or the plane John Travolta flies. It's the thought in your head that says, "Why can't I have that? Without it, my life is so incomplete."

The fruit is always something outside your reach.

The serpent, on the other hand, represents a new and dangerous form of insatiable hunger. He points out Adam and Eve's deficiencies, making them feel incomplete and inadequate. Thanks to him, for the first time Adam and Eve have to look for material objects to fill the void.

After the serpent dangles that apple in front of Eve, all of her satisfaction with life turns to despair. She becomes fixated on satisfying her urges. Eve moves away from ordinary human hunger, and indulgence becomes the order of the day. *Unrequited desire is now consuming her, and all she can think about is satisfying her lust.*

I once counseled a wealthy businessman named Jeremy who was loyal to his wife but felt that he suffered from never-ending lust. "You don't know what sacrifices I make to be faithful," he said to me. "There are so many women. So many. And they're interested in me, flirt with me, and make it known that they're available. I suffer so much."

I told him that I found it fascinating that he found hunger to be a form of suffering. "Isn't the whole reason you're successful because you hunger? While others are satisfied with a nine-to-five job, your hunger for great success led you to be an entrepreneur. And while others would have been satisfied starting one successful business, you sold that one and started another. Now you're telling me that hungering for women is something that is supposed to be indulged and the only reason you don't is that you don't want to cheat on your wife. On the contrary, this lust you have for the feminine is supposed to be redirected toward your beautiful wife so that you never get bored in your marriage. You simply have to learn how to harness hunger in your marriage."

The story of Eve and the serpent began an endless historical cycle of consumption in human history, with people rejecting the urge to hunger. Humanity, after being evicted from the Garden, pursued a path of sensual indulgence, forever seeking to satisfy every desire, to indulge every whim. From Alexander the Great to Napoleon to so many in between, humanity has demonstrated that even all of the earth is not enough to satisfy their hunger. And now, as we consume all of the oil, coal, and mineral wealth the world has to offer, we are demonstrating that our never-ending quest for complete satiation knows no bounds.

We should know better. We're not supposed to fill ourselves with every last material object until we are stuffed to the brim. And we're not supposed to have sex with every available partner until we've lost the capacity to share true intimacy. Everyone knows this innately, even if we often choose to satiate ourselves rather than act on that knowledge.

Yet here's the part that will surprise you: *give the serpent his due.* That's right. Even the serpent has seeds of holiness. He is tapping into a genuine human need. He understands that the real enemy of humankind is complacency. He knows that human beings dare not stagnate. Their curiosity, their desire to expand, to want, to know, their essential unrequited desire is their greatest strength. By offering up a forbidden treat, he taps into a genuine human need, twisting it just enough to catch us off guard.

Hunger is not only real, it's an essential and natural impulse. The serpent's true genius was tricking Eve into thinking that hunger was merely an itch to be scratched. The serpent convinced Eve that her goal in life should be to expand herself horizontally. His voice—which is identical to society's voice today—whispered in her ear, "You want more possessions, more success, more fame. More sexual conquests."

Does it never occur to us that perhaps hunger is meant to linger in perpetuity? That maybe hunger exists to push us to rise to greater heights and achieve ever-greater things? What if we get hungry in order to expand not horizontally, but vertically? To become wiser, to go ever deeper, to lift ourselves higher? The truth is that we are supposed to *hunger* in life in these ways, not merely satiate ourselves. I hold that satisfying ourselves is precisely what we should *not* be doing. Instead, we should all embrace our hunger for greater things.

The first step to taking back hunger is looking in the mirror and using your inner voice of inspiration to conduct an unflinchingly honest self-talk. As you gaze at yourself, speak the truth and say,

> From the stuff I eat that's not healthy for me, to all of the Sundays spent at shopping malls rather than at a park or on a hike, to all of the stupid, mind-numbing TV I watch, which prevents me from ever having a proper conversation with my spouse, *I've got to stop filling my life up with junk.*
>
> True as it is of my appetite for food, it applies to my marriage as well. I used to have such a deep sexual hunger for my spouse. Now, whenever I feel a sexual need, I immediately satisfy it with quickie sex that fulfills neither of us. The same is true with masturbation, which I recognize is nothing more than a means to simply purge sexual desire within me. I have to learn, when I'm feeling lustful, to sometimes just hug my spouse and fall asleep in his/her arms. To delay physical gratification so that its steam can build and we can then have the magic of lust restored to our marriage as the Tantric masters have taught [about which I write a great deal in my book *The Kosher Sutra*].

It's not easy to say this to yourself, but in doing so, you're using your inner voice of inspiration to silence the ceaseless voices in modern culture that urge you to spend as if there is no end, shop till you drop, and watch TV until you pass out.

It is but the first step on your journey to letting your inner voice be the guide to a new and ravenous hunger for greater things.

In this country, it seems we've found a perfect cocktail of unhealthy remedies for human hunger—whether it's Hollywood fiction, so that we always live in someone else's story; whether it's pornography, so that we get to have a sexual climax without sexual intimacy; or whether, as seems to happen most frequently of all, it turns out to be food.

So many Americans gorge themselves on potato chips, desserts, and fast foods of all kinds (at times, I, too, am one of those Americans). Of the many examples of the phenomenon of denying hunger that I can give, overeating is the most straightforward and yet the most profound. America rejects hunger—and we have the expanding waistlines to prove it.

When you find yourself opening the refrigerator one too many times, you need to ask yourself a question: "Am I a person who resorts to self-indulgence every time I sense that my belly isn't quite full? Or do I have the potential to be something better, someone with the willpower and the wherewithal to resist my urges?" Answer from the heart: "*I refuse to satiate myself with comfort food*; my life could amount to so much more if I redirected my hunger toward greater things!"

For many people, the impulse to gorge themselves springs from unsatisfied emotional hunger within. I once counseled a man named Timothy. He and his wife, Laura, had three children and were living a happy life. But there was a catch. Laura had grown up in a financially strapped household and couldn't face living in poverty again. During the economic downturn, Timothy lost his job, and Laura flipped. She said, "You know what? I'm sorry, I know this is wrong, but this is not what I signed up for. I can't do this." And she left him. She was a pretty, charismatic woman looking for a guy with means, and soon enough she found one. The guy had no children, but he loved kids, and it wasn't long before she had moved in, and all of her children started calling him Dad!

As you can imagine, Timothy was crushed. After Laura left, he put on a significant amount of weight. When I went to counsel him, he was large—very large. He told me, "I hate the way I look, I hate myself, I'm miserable, and it's all because my kids are calling some other guy Dad . . . I feel like there's nothing left for me."

Obviously, he was eating to bury his pain. Yet above all else, he had lost touch with his real appetite. Like all men and women, Timothy had a hunger to be important, to be *necessary* to the world and especially to his own children. When that hunger was left unattended, he papered over the void with a shallower consumption. What else can we expect from a culture that finds it easier to satisfy hunger with unhealthy distractions than to embrace that hunger and the yearning for something deeper?

All men and women hunger to be necessary. The great Jewish thinker Maimonides distinguished between a contingent, inessential existence and a necessary existence. We all yearn for the latter. But Timothy was necessary to no one. He used to support his wife and children. He used to come home and his children would throw their arms around him. Now someone else was acting like a father to them. Timothy had been replaced utterly. So he transformed that hunger into a literal hunger. This is precisely why we must explore the essential difference between horizontal and vertical hunger, lest we fall into the trap that ensnared Timothy's appetite.

We all hunger; that fact of life will never change. The question is for what, and whether we do so vertically or horizontally. The quintessential posture of the dead is horizontal. The dead and the sleeping are the only humans who don't hunger. And animals hunger only for that which is below them; their posture makes them look at the ground. When humans are alive and awake, however, our natural posture is vertical. We look to the heavens. We're supposed to indulge our hunger in the quest for wisdom, understanding the secrets of ourselves and of the universe, going deeper into our own souls, our minds, and our God.

The best example of a collision between the two hungers is found in the story of Alexander the Great and Diogenes the Cynic. Alexander was the archetype of those who hunger horizontally. After a childhood in which his philandering father, Phillip II, left his mother for another woman, Alexander was forced to grow up in competition with his half siblings. As a young man, he was plagued with tremendous insecurities and was determined to prove himself.

He acquired an insatiable hunger for power and fame. All of the earth was not enough to sate his horizontal lust. As a military leader, he became the model for every other power-hungry man who followed him—Caesar, Genghis Khan, Napoleon. No wonder: Alexander was the first to conquer the world on horseback.

It is said that when Alexander heard that the philosopher Diogenes was the smartest person in the world, he decided he must meet the man. So he went to Corinth, where Diogenes was contemplating his theories as he lay in the sun. Alexander stood over him and said, "I am Alexander, conqueror of worlds; put forward your request and it shall be done." Diogenes squinted up at him, shook his head, and said, "Just get out of my light."

What Diogenes was really saying to Alexander was: "What could *you* possibly do for *me*? You live in a different realm. Yours is a horizontal modality. But mine is purely vertical. I yearn for deep thought, philosophy, books, and wisdom. I'm not so insecure that I need anything from you. So just get out of my light. *I'm trying to ascend vertically*; I'm trying to think here! I'm fathoming universes while you have this petty conversation with me."

It's crucial to maintain Diogenes' vertical hunger in your life. If you engage your inner voice of inspiration, it will remind you of the time when you still heeded that vertical hunger. Start a self-talk to remind yourself and say,

> I remember how much hungrier I was as a child. I felt so curious about everything around me. I used to ask so many questions. From the shape of clouds to the animals and plants, all things were engaging.
>
> I remember how much I loved reading books. I remember looking out the car window as my family took long drives. I found the trees and the leaves endlessly fascinating.
>
> My own children still have this hunger. They ask so many questions, but I deflect them with trite nonsense. I find their questions tiresome and intrusive. It's a pain. It seems that all I want

is for them to be quiet so I can make a phone call in the car, listen to the radio, or watch my favorite TV show.

It's clear that I've lost my intellectual and emotional hunger. It's been so long since I went to a great class, read a challenging book, or had a deep conversation with my spouse about the direction and purpose of my life. Even when I go to synagogue or church, it seems perfunctory. I'm discharging an obligation, rather than hungering to really connect with God. I'm allowing my mind to rot.

It's time to change my life's course. *I will choose a vertical hunger over a horizontal hunger.*

It's truly admirable to make this declaration—but it is, nonetheless, one of many self-talks you must have. There are still other appetites that you must confront, and the next one may hit you right where it hurts the most: your pocketbook.

In our lives today, it seems the only thing we really care about is cash—how much we're making, what we're buying with it, and when we can get more. Yet when it comes to things that really matter, we make do with so little. We're okay going through life with little knowledge of the history that defines us. We're okay working nine-to-five jobs that neither bring out our best qualities nor force us to take risks. We're even okay with marriages where sex happens at best once a week for no more than ten minutes. Hey, at least we're still having it, right? And if we sense a void inside us, a feeling that we are somehow unfulfilled, what better solution than to head for the mall for a little retail therapy?

It is all too easy to be deceived by the voice of our consumerist culture. Magazines, television, advertisements—all of them barrage us, urging us to buy expensive clothes, acquire meaningless objects, and spend our money as soon as we get it. Materialism is truly one of our society's most dangerous hungers. Left unchecked, it can wreck our lives.

I have found that this kind of profligacy is often a substitution for another hunger. I once met a woman named Natalie who was desperate for affection from her husband, Mark. He loved his kids, but he never really played with them, nor did he put in any time with them. Similarly, he said he loved Natalie, but he never showed it. They never had real conversations. He was always at a distance, and her hunger for intimacy, for a deep and fulfilling connection with a soul mate, was left to languish unfulfilled.

How did Natalie respond? By spending crazy amounts of money. When she bought a new handbag, it would literally make her happy for days. She'd show it to everyone and talk about little else, saying bluntly, "*This* is what makes me happy." My response was that this sort of thing is what makes kids happy! If you give a child a trinket, the child is temporarily satisfied. That isn't and shouldn't be true for adults. And yet, to a great extent, our inability to hunger properly has made us all into children.

We all know people like Natalie. Some of us may even recognize her characteristics in ourselves. If we are to advance in life and convert our baser impulses into greater things, we must interrogate ourselves, taking on our inner voice in fierce debate. Ask yourself:

Where did my hunger go? As soon as there is money in my pocket, I've already spent it—and on what? Nothing of value. My problem seems to be that I no longer hunger for a better life. The petty, short-term satisfaction of material goods has served to keep me distracted from the legitimate hungers I have neglected. I have become all too complacent.

In place of self-development, it seems that I hunger only for information about other people. I have become a Facebook addict, constantly searching out other people's updates. I devour *People* magazine and *Us Weekly* to find out what Angelina Jolie wore to the Oscars.

I no longer hunger to read classic literature, to understand what's going on in the world, to discipline myself and become a better person. I'm ashamed to admit that my hunger to raise wonderful children has dwindled as well—all I am left with is a compulsion to satiate myself with material goods, comfort food, and short-term stimulation. Well, no more. *I intend to embrace hunger anew.*

Instead of throwing my money away on material things, I'm going to make something of it. I'm going to embrace hunger, save, and even give to charity when I can. The way that I spend will be one more opportunity to change the course of my life.

Our lives are nothing but a short span of time. And if we spend tons of time earning money that we simply throw away, then we're throwing away part of our potential.

A friend of mine named Tom is an incredibly humble man who happens to be a hedge fund manager making hundreds of millions of dollars every year. He could easily throw in the towel and kick back on a tropical island for the rest of his life. But not Tom.

I once asked him, "What motivates you to keep working? Don't you already have it all?" His response was that when he gets to the office every morning, there are already thirty messages waiting for him from charities, requesting that he contribute. He shook his head, saying, "If I made thirty billion dollars, it still wouldn't be enough." And so, Tom works and works and gives and gives. He has enough money to live comfortably, and then he gives away more than a third of what he makes. His hunger is always there.

It only stands to reason: once you have it all, what is there left to hunger for? Say you have the Maybach, the yacht, the private plane, the mansion, and a harem of pretty girls—what's left to live for? That's when people start turning to drugs, because nothing in life can satisfy them anymore.

Keep Tom's hunger to give in the back of your mind, and act in kind. Spend your money on things of real, lasting value—and save the rest. If you do so, your hunger will never burn out.

Perhaps the most important relationship in your life is that between you and your spouse—and hunger is absolutely necessary to keep that connection alive. I maintain that the death of marriage is nothing more than the loss of hunger. Yet even when the spark of love in a marriage seems to have been extinguished, all that some couples need is a little push to renew their hunger for each other.

Don and Stacy had been married for about eleven years when they came to see me. Don had lost all hunger for his wife. He thought their conversations had become boring, and he claimed that she was much more interested in the children than in him. Clearly, something needed to wake him up. So, in front of Don, I asked Stacy, "Are you lonely in your marriage?"

"Desperately," she said.

"How long have you been lonely?"

"Probably two to three years."

As Don sat uncomfortably next to her, I told her, "There's not a man alive who can't spot a lonely wife from far away. Male astronauts can spot them from space. So let me ask you this: is there a man who's been showing you a lot of attention?"

At this, she froze up. "I can't really discuss this in front of my husband." Yet after I asked again, she finally admitted, "Well, there is a guy at work, but it's completely innocent between us. We talk, we giggle, he tells me about the things I missed on TV the night before because I was taking care of the kids. What's so wrong with that?"

"Have you ever felt sexually attracted to this man? Have you ever fantasized about him sexually?" About three minutes passed in silence before she nodded her head. "How often?"

"Not that often," she said. "Maybe two or three times."

Here's the interesting thing, though: her husband was originally devastated by the prospect of a new man in her life. But in the long term, this discovery reawakened his interest, albeit in a very painful way. *It kindled in him a new hunger for her.*

So, why didn't he hunger for her in the first place? Well, as far as he was concerned, she had become monolithic. She was nothing but a cook and a cleaner, seemingly uninterested in sex or in intellectual pursuits of any kind. He couldn't follow her through her transition from woman to wife, wife to mom. When he discovered that he actually knew nothing about her, his curiosity was completely reawakened. It came in a painful way, but eroticism and pain are inextricably linked.

If you engage your inner voice of inspiration in a serious bout of self-talk, you will admit the truth about your own life. Say to yourself,

When my spouse and I first dated, I wanted to know everything about her/him. We talked and talked, and we never got bored. I was so hungry that I wanted to spend the rest of my life with this person. I could never have enough.

Now that hunger has been stymied by the endless noise of the TV. And in the bedroom, no less. I watch so late into the night that I wake up tired most mornings. I have to admit it, I'm an addict. I'll watch things that I'm not really even interested in. I'll channel surf through endless coma-inducing programs. I find it soothing. It makes me forget my responsibilities and problems. It fills the emptiness. Yes, it quenches my hunger.

But I now understand—hunger is crucial to our relationship, and I must commit myself to finding it anew. The survival of my marriage hangs in the balance.

It's not only you—our entire society seems to array its forces to stamp out hunger in marriage. In 2003, a woman from Texas named Joanne was hosting "passion parties," gatherings where she gave sex advice, offered up lingerie, and generally counseled other women from her church. The result: she was kicked out of her church and arrested for indecency. I thought this was utterly ridiculous; what could be wrong with advocating for husbands and wives to have a deeper sexual connection?

I invited Joanne onto my radio show to discuss her story. To represent the opposing viewpoint, I invited my friend the Reverend Flip Benham from Operation Rescue to comment.

I asked Flip, "What did Joanne do wrong?"

Flip jumped in—"Shmuley, she was trying to make men objectify and lust after their wives."

I was shocked. "Flip," I said, "are you seriously suggesting that you don't lust after your own wife?"

He demurred, "Absolutely not. I would never turn my wife into an object. I feel sorry for your wife, Shmuley. You've made her into an object." In response, I asked him if he knew the tenth commandment. "Of course I do," he told me. "It's 'thou shalt not covet thy neighbor's wife.'"

"This is exactly my point. The tenth commandment is telling us that the right thing to do is not to lust after *other* men's wives—but to lust after your own wife. If the commandment meant for you to do otherwise, it would have asked you not to lust after any woman at all. Lusting after your wife is not only natural but necessary and condoned by God Himself. Lust and hunger in marriage are holy."

Naturally, there should be contentment in marriage and intimacy as well. But no marriage can survive without passion, which is the opposite of contentment.

To save your marriage, you need to come up with ways to create hunger for your spouse. Sometimes, sexual separation is the key. In the Jewish religion, a married couple separates sexually for the five days of menstruation and the seven days afterward. This period is called *Niddah*. The principal reason? *So that there will be hunger.* Instead of instantaneously satisfying our desires, we should instead build a dam against them. Relationship experts call it "the erotic obstacle," something I wrote about extensively in my book *The Kosher Sutra*. If we do this, our hunger can build up until it overcomes the dam like a river in flood. This is the essence of embracing hunger and a crucial step in preserving the erotic spark in your relationship.

So, strike up a self-talk and admit the truth by saying to yourself:

I want to embrace hunger and learn to lust after my spouse again. We love each other, but I freely admit that the lust is gone. There was a time when we couldn't keep our hands off each other, when every inch of our bodies and our being was terrain for endless exploration. Now we both get into bed at night, and it's barely a minute before either the TV is blaring or one of us is asleep. The direct consequence is that so much of the excitement in our lives has been lost. And maybe that's why we watch so much TV in the bedroom, to fill the void of monotony and boredom.

One of the first things I'll do to embrace hunger in my marriage is get the TV out of the bedroom. Our bedroom is too private, too intimate, to be invaded by external forces. My connection with my spouse is too precious, too important, to be overtaken by artificial entertainment.

I'm going to elevate the level of conversation between me and my spouse. From now on, 10 p.m. and afterward will be a function-free zone in our relationship. Nothing practical will be discussed—only the emotional and the intellectual. I want to ask my spouse whether he/she is satisfied with our life, what dreams we still have to explore, and what he/she thinks life has taught us during the last year. My marriage is too holy, our connection too deep and spiritual, for me to be satisfied with it as a mere partnership.

And in the process of learning to explore my spouse anew, I'll make a real effort to get know him/her on a deeper level. I'm going to find a place in his/her mind, penetrate his/her heart, and discover my spouse anew.

If you are vertically hungry and guided by your inner voice of inspiration, you will always be fulfilled by enriching your life with new relationships, experiences, ideas, and books. If you have vertical emptiness, you will seek horizontal happiness, and you will never be full.

If we embrace hunger, we will not feel as if we have to satisfy every yearning and every lust. A married man who lusts after a stranger is supposed to keep on hungering, rather than seek to satisfy an illicit urge. It is precisely this hunger that will lead him back to his wife. A child who is given three meals a day is not supposed to snack in between. Keeping him from obesity means teaching him to embrace hunger. Not every urge exists to be satisfied, and not every whim is meant to be indulged. On the contrary, the more we embrace hunger, the higher we will eventually reach. But the more we focus on satisfying our lust, the less frequently that lust will propel us to achieve our goals. So let hunger retake its place of prominence in our lives, and we can rekindle the greatest vertical hunger of all: the hunger for spirituality.

If you ask your inner voice, it will answer. Say to yourself,

When I was a child, I always wondered about God. Where was He? How big was He? And did He really care about all of His human children? I want to rediscover that Godly hunger. I want more of God in my life, because I recognize that God is the source of all real hunger. That in His infinite expansiveness He affords an endless journey. That the real source of all true longing is the human desire to attach ourselves to something infinite.

I know that to hunger for God, I have to hunger for more of His revealed truth. I have to start reading the Bible on a regular basis. I remember reading how Abraham Lincoln, at the height of the Civil War, turned to the pages of the Bible on a daily basis for inspiration when it seemed that his cause was lost. I know that hungering for God also means giving more to charity and spending less money on myself, giving at least 5 and hopefully even 10 percent of my annual income to the needy. The more I hunger to make an impact in the lives of others, the less content I will be with satisfying only my needs.

Furthermore, I can't kindle this hunger alone. I will commit myself to seeking expert guidance in my path back to God. I will return to church/synagogue, no matter how long it's been since I last attended. They will be happy to receive me again and delighted to assist me in the service of my insatiable spiritual hunger. I will enroll myself in Bible study groups and classes on the great religious texts. Every new step will make me ever hungrier for spiritual fulfillment.

And, in the end, all of these hungers will lead me back to love, because God is love.

If you listen closely to the voice of inspiration, it will tell you:

I have lived long enough to know that there is nothing in life so special as love. To love and be loved. To give love and receive love. I recognize that I am the product of a wayward culture that substitutes people's hunger for love with a hunger for things. It claims that objects, rather than people, bring real satisfaction—that a man can be on his fifth marriage, but if he owns a private jet and a yacht he is still called a success and others seek to emulate him. I will never make the same mistake.

I remember so well what Victor Frankl said about love in his moving classic *Man's Search for Meaning*. Writing about the hopelessness he felt as an inmate in Auschwitz, he suddenly thought of his wife and was redeemed.

A thought transfixed me: for the first time in my life I saw the truth as it is set into song by so many poets, proclaimed as the final wisdom by so many thinkers. The truth—that love is the ultimate and the highest goal to which man can aspire. Then I grasped the meaning of the greatest secret that human poetry and human thought and belief have to impart: *The salvation of man is through love and in love.* I understood how a man who has nothing left in this world still may know bliss, be it only for a brief moment, in the contemplation of his beloved. In a position of utter desolation, when man cannot express himself in positive action, when his only achievement may consist in enduring his sufferings in the right way—an honorable way—in such a position man can, through loving contemplation of the image he carries of his beloved, achieve fulfillment. For the first time in my life I was able to understand the meaning of the words, *The angels are lost in perpetual contemplation of an infinite glory.*

I, too, wish to know that glory. I, too, wish to rediscover love.
Say to yourself,

Yes, I *will* embrace hunger. I'm too young and my potential is too precious to allow my life to pass me by without really living. I realize that those who do not hunger are as the dead. And I refuse to allow my existence to become like that of the living dead.

I will no longer be satisfied with the superficial objects that my culture puts before me as objects of desire. Yes, I want money, and yes, I want professional achievements. As with anyone, recognition is important to me. But much more important is the lifelong quest for meaning and purpose. And I now understand that it is a journey without end. *Hunger is a positive and perpetual state.*

I want to be intellectually curious. And I know that real intellectual hunger is also a lifelong pursuit. The oracle at Delphi said that Socrates was the wisest of all men because he was the only one who knew that he did not know. And Kabbalah's principal text, the *Zohar*, says that real knowledge is coming to the realization of what you cannot know. I want to peer into the infinite, into the endless expanse of the unknowable, so that my hunger remains utterly unsatisfied and my thirst utterly unquenched.

Over and over, say to yourself, "Through learning to hunger again, I will be born anew."

To develop a personalized relationship with your inner voice of inspiration, ask yourself the following questions. Respond to them, and let the answers guide you on self-talks of your own devising.

Am I satisfied with superficial responses to things? When my kids ask me questions, do I blow them off, or do I stoke our collective hunger for knowledge?

Do I read? Could I read more, attend lectures or cultural events, or engage my friends and my spouse in conversations about the deeper currents in our lives and in our culture?

When I watch the news or read the paper, do I simply take note of what is happening, or do I ask myself why things are the way they are and investigate further?

Do I eat constantly whenever I get the urge? Do I have quickie sex with my spouse that squelches my appetite but also diminishes our connection?

In sum, am I consulting with my inner voice of inspiration to change my behavior, and am I truly embracing hunger?

2

Choose Love, Not Attention

CONVERSATION 2
I will use self-talk to remind myself of the difference
between unconditional acceptance and painful insecurity.

Never before in history has there been a generation less sure
about its place in the world than ours. Yet our insecurity is not
merely about fluctuations in the stock market, oil spills in the Gulf of
Mexico, or wars raging in the Middle East. Our generation exhibits a
deeper anxiety, as if we're not content simply to be ourselves.

Subject to wild mood swings, we find it supremely challenging
to maintain successful relationships. We pick fights, allow ourselves to
be divided politically, and seem to choose friends who suit our chosen identity, instead of being open to all people and ideas.

Fundamentally, we seem to live externally, rather than internally.
To define ourselves, we lean on our possessions, degrees, acquain-
tances, and neighborhoods. Identity itself is like a suit we slide into in

order to give our lives meaning. It is inevitable, therefore, when this suit begins to irritate us as being foreign and uncomfortable.

So, what's happening to us?

I don't want to discount the many complex and important factors that contribute to insecurity, materialism, and superficiality. Tumultuous changes have occurred in our society during the last century, and our media culture has played no small part in the shift as well. Yet the overarching source is a void within us—one that we strive constantly, but not altogether successfully, to fill.

This void is the absence of the one vital ingredient that validates our uniqueness more than anything else: love.

It begins when we're little kids—at a crucial stage in our development, we fail to receive from our parents the love and attention we need. Maybe it's all of the electronic intrusions in the house. Parents love their kids but at times seem a bit bored with them, and thus may feel a need to distract themselves with electronic gadgets. They cherish their children but fail to sufficiently interact with them. Studies show that dads tend to give no more than three minutes of uninterrupted quality time to their kids per day. Another survey reveals that a full fifth of middle school and high school students report that they haven't had a good conversation that lasted more than ten minutes with either of their parents in *more than a month*.

> *It's not that our parents don't love us—they certainly do,*
> *infinitely. But love does not translate into engagement.*

We are raised with so many distractions that our sense of our own uniqueness becomes fragile. A void opens within, and we settle for love's counterfeit cousin, attention.

What's the end result of this deficiency? Take two of my friends, Jimmy and Roger, who represent the two different approaches to love and attention.

Jimmy owns a small gardening company and clears about $250,000 a year. A humble man, if you ask him what he does for a living, he'll tell you that he has a company that cuts people's grass. He dresses modestly and never seeks to be the center of attention. He has easy conversations with anyone who is seated next to him at social functions and remains calm at all times. He happens to have a famous sister who is a singer, but he rarely reveals that fact unless it comes up organically in a conversation. If you happen to run into Jimmy, you'll invariably walk away admiring him for his sincerity, warmth, and humility.

Roger is a different kind of guy. It's not that he isn't wholesome; it's just that he is usually angling for something. If he's ever helped you out, you can bet that one day he'll expect a favor in return. Like a heat-seeking missile, he is drawn to the influential and powerful guests at any social event. He lives for celebrity gossip and knows everything happening in the private life of virtually any stratospherically rich or famous person in America. He's happy to tell you about it.

Which of my friends, Jimmy or Roger, would you rather get to know? More important, which one is more like you? Think carefully, because the answer will settle the question: *is your life all about love, or is it about attention?*

If you find yourself hesitating, engage your inner voice of inspiration in self-talk and say,

> I know it's time to be honest with myself. I've been wondering whether the impulses that drive and animate me are healthy. I seem inordinately preoccupied with what others think of me. Even the most superficial things—how I look, how I'm dressed—can stop me in my tracks. Sometimes I won't even go to synagogue or church services because I don't have the right clothes to wear. In my heart I know that life is not a popularity contest. Still, I spend an inordinate amount of time trying to get people to like me.

I have a religious Jewish friend named Mordechai who grew up in a Hassidic community. At age eighteen, he was walking down the main thoroughfare when he became conscious of the fact that he was wearing blue pants, thereby breaking the unspoken all-black dress code. He worried that others might be staring at him. He decided then and there that the community was not right for him. He eventually, and rather rapidly, abandoned his Jewish observance and moved out of the community. Today, he is spiritually lost and estranged from his family. What he should have done, I told him, was focus on being authentically observant, rather than care about what people thought of him. By getting caught up in externalities, he threw out the baby with the bathwater and gave up a precious tradition that has kept millions wholesome and spiritually grounded for three thousand years.

That's why we have to talk to ourselves about being more inwardly directed.

In a conversation with your inner voice of inspiration, say,

In intimate relationships, such as my marriage, I don't always stand up for myself. I allow my own needs to go unattended. I give and rarely receive. Virtuous as it is to be so giving, and happy as I am not to be a taker, I have to be honest about what's really going on under the surface. *My behavior is the manifestation of deep-seated insecurities.*

The source of this insecurity is clear: I am haunted by a feeling of overarching inadequacy. My life is plagued by a feeling of never enough, never enough, never enough. And the result? I allow my boss to push me around because I fear I'm not capable of getting a better job. I kowtow to my spouse, though I know our relationship should be on an even footing. I even allow my own children to take advantage of me—I'm so desperate for their love that I capitulate to their every desire. For any of these people to think less of me is too painful to contemplate.

But no more. *From now on I will choose love, not attention.*

Now that we've talked about the lack of love, we need to ask, Where does this need for attention come from?

Humans have always sought to establish their own uniqueness and specialness. Just look at world history: it has been said that the first person who became truly famous was Alexander the Great. He chased after glory, as well as power, and brought chroniclers along on his campaigns to ensure that his exploits would live on in posterity. A few centuries later, Emperor Augustus took cues from Alexander, spreading his fame even more widely by having his own visage stamped on coins. That way, even his illiterate Roman subjects could look at his picture and know who he was. Over the centuries, men and women continued to add themselves to this pantheon of famous names, reaching a climax with Charles Lindbergh, who historians say was the first globally famous man of the twentieth century. Since Lindbergh's time, however, there has been a sea change in what it means to be famous.

From Alexander the Great to Charles Lindbergh, the fundamental quality that defined celebrity was bold accomplishment. Lindbergh, while unfortunately a Hitler-admiring anti-Semite, was famous for his courage, Augustus for his leadership, Alexander for his valor. Attention served to magnify virtue; celebrity enhanced dignity. These men became famous because of something that the public at the time thought admirable about them. Times have changed. Ours is the first generation to put celebrity and dignity in direct conflict. We're the first people in human history who are prepared to sacrifice our honor in the pursuit of short-lived fame. Many of us are delighted—even eager—to be exploited by TV producers, humiliating ourselves on national television. A producer asks us to eat dung on *Fear Factor*, talk about our sexual trysts in intimate detail on *The Real World*, expose our family's dirty laundry on *Supernanny*, and we think nothing of agreeing to do this. It just shows you how desperate we are for attention: we are prepared to lose our dignity to acquire celebrity.

In previous generations, Paris Hilton, Charlie Sheen, Lindsay Lohan, or any other badly behaved star would have hidden his or her deficiencies—today we revel in them. Even Michael Jackson, a tremendously talented performer and musician and a person for whom

I cared deeply, lived through the tragedy of seeing his talent become subordinate to notoriety for bizarre behavior.

People used to hide their flaws. Now they become famous precisely because *of them.*

What we need to be saying to ourselves in self-talk is simple: "I have nothing to prove, but I do have something to contribute. My ambition is not to make my mark but to contribute my gift. I must choose love, rather than attention." We must enunciate these words without reservations of any kind, and even more urgently, we need to help our children learn to say them from the very beginning.

The scars of a generation that lives for attention rather than love are all around us. From hookup culture to kids' seeming reluctance to even spend time with their parents, it seems there is an outright epidemic of attention-seeking behavior. And whom do we have to blame for this state of affairs but ourselves? We have shown our children that they need to perform to get love. Not long ago, I observed as my friend Mary Anne's daughter Jill told her about an essay she'd written on Thomas Jefferson. The eleven-year-old was proud of herself for receiving a B for her efforts. So was her mom—sort of. "A B is great, honey," she said, "but you're smart enough to get an A next time." All that her daughter heard was, "I'm really proud of you, honey. But if you get an A, I'll be even more proud. You'll be even more special to me."

I call this phenomenon Mafia Love. "Make me an offer I can't refuse, child. Become so compelling that I cannot help but love you." The lesson is that love must be earned. Mafia Love has turned love into a quantity both finite and conditional; little wonder that after we have put a price on affection, our children are reluctant to spend their own love on us in return.

Parents seem dead set on conditioning their children to date the right sort of people, to marry based on social status, and to do whatever it takes to get into the "best" university. My least favorite manifestation of this phenomenon: parents who teach their kids to suck up to teachers.

As important as education is, I've never told my children that they need to be valedictorian—character is so much more vital. At Oxford, I saw firsthand how many of the brightest students chose to play it safe, subordinating happiness to success. They began by cultivating friendships with all of the right professors, and they lived their lives so conditioned to succeed that they were not prepared to risk anything of value.

Matthew, a student with whom I was close at Oxford, used to make a beeline for all of the students who came from prestigious families. Once, at the Oxford Union bar, I saw him laughing uncontrollably at the jokes of the son of the prime minister of a European nation. It was sad to witness because Matthew had so much to offer as a friend, rather than as a suck-up. But he was convinced that he could get by only through attaching himself to the right people. He often told me, "It's not what you know but who you know." Now that he works as a money manager for superwealthy clients, he is always nervous about what they think of him. He is a rich man, and I recently asked him, "Isn't wealth supposed to be liberating? If it is, then it's strange to see that you are one of the most imprisoned people I know. You are terrified about whether your clients still like you."

These are the students who might end up rising to a position of advising the president, yet never run for office themselves. Why would they ever take that kind of risk when they might fail? It takes true character to take a real risk—look, for instance, at innovators such as Larry Ellison, Steve Jobs, Mark Zuckerberg, or Bill Gates, who dropped out of school altogether in the interest of contributing their gifts to the world. I don't advocate doing the same, of course. Education is tremendously important. But just imagine the level of self-confidence these entrepreneurs had when they left institutions such as Harvard because they had their own personal dreams and did not believe they needed something external to establish them.

A few months ago, I saw a classic example of a non–risk taker in action. I was attending a friend's daughter's high school graduation.

Midway through the ceremony, the valedictorian was introduced in the most glowing terms. The principal praised her, and when the applause died down, she began her speech. What did she tell us? That this was the greatest school ever, that each of her teachers was the most inspiring ever, that each and every subject she took and the ideas she learned were the most life-changing ever. Look, I'm sure she got great grades, but it was one of the worst speeches I've ever heard. It was nothing but a public celebration of her insecurity and her need to patronize teachers whom she was desperate to impress.

As I listened to the speech, I couldn't help but think of how her behavior reflected on her teachers and parents. They had managed to instill in this otherwise bright young adult the idea that only status and grades matter. What a mistake! The goal is not to create students who brown-nose every teacher in school. We need to create intellectually inquisitive adults who challenge their teachers. Never allow yourself to become a shallow sycophant.

It's imperative that parents engage in self-talk about these issues:

I sense that my desire for my children to succeed is beginning to overpower everything else in our relationship. I want so badly for them to do well that it's blinding me to what I'm really doing: *I'm making my child jump through hoops in order to win my affection.* Even if it is the way I was raised, even if it's difficult to change course, I know that I'm only instilling in my children the habit of defining themselves externally. I need to remember to compliment them, rather than criticize. I need to express my love and pride in their achievements openly and often. Because if I only tell my kids that they're not good enough, then they're never going to feel that they are!

As a father, I have to take care not to make that same error. It's so easy to walk into a messy room and berate your children for every little mistake they've made in failing to clean up. Yet if I act on this impulse, castigating my children at a moment's notice, they will swiftly begin to think, first, that all I ever do is criticize them, and second, that their father is a pain to be around. We all make mistakes—but we also have to own up to them. How else can we teach our children to differentiate between love and attention?

A few years ago on a Jewish fast day, I took my younger children out in the afternoon to make the day easier on my wife. My older daughters were going to make dinner for everyone once the sun set and it was time to break the fast. I got home shortly before it was time to eat—but nothing was ready. No one had had any food or water for a full day, and now there was nothing to eat.

I flew off the handle. "You acted selfishly," I said to my daughters. "Everyone's starving because of your poor planning. How could you?"

Yet even as the words came out of my mouth, I could see my daughters shutting down in front of me. They had a perspective all their own: they were fasting, too, moving more slowly than normal, and sure, they were running a few minutes behind schedule, but they'd still managed to get started, and dinner was on the way. If it was going to be twenty minutes late, then their dad should hold his tongue and be patient.

And you know what? They were right.

I swallowed my pride and immediately said to them, "I made a mistake and I'm sorry. Next time I'd appreciate it if you would start dinner just a little earlier, but I'm fully responsible for my own inappropriate outburst. I apologize for hurting you. The lesson for all of us is that just because one person is hungry, it doesn't give him the license to shout at everyone else. I love you guys, and I need to curb myself when I get upset for petty reasons."

All of us parents need to remember that our own insecurities and feelings of inadequacy spring directly from our complex childhoods. Not only that, these insecurities can all too easily be passed on to our own children. Engage yourself in conversation, and discover the root of your doubts and confusions:

In being honest with myself, I have to admit that this sense of inadequacy and insecurity comes from an absence of love.

I know my parents loved me. And I know they would do any-thing for me. But they just didn't show it enough.

My father was a good man, but he had such intimacy issues—he found it incredibly difficult just to say that he loved me. And my mother, she was very affectionate, but she was also stern. I even felt at times that she was competitive with me in certain areas—perhaps that she even resented me for having opportunities that she never had. And they were both so busy all of the time.

They worked so hard to support us and give us a good life, but it did take its toll. I remember when I was young that I'd have to ask my father the same question four times just to get an answer from him. I was always competing for his attention. And then there were some things that happened that really bothered me. My father missed so many school plays and so many parent-teacher nights. And was it so difficult to compliment me? When I showed that I got a B on a really difficult science exam, did my parents have to say, "If you try harder, you can get an A"?

I'm not here to fault my parents. Even less do I wish to play the victim. Although my parents were not perfect, they did so many other things right. Rather, I'm examining all of these things for the self-awareness and self-understanding they pro-vide for me.

I understand that I, like so many others, was deprived of love. And my childhood was just the beginning. The tortured relationships that followed, the fighting I did with some of my siblings—it all made me feel deprived of love. And when you're deprived of love, you're deprived of a sense of adequacy, of being enough, of being sufficient.

Since I'm not a victim, it's time for me to heal. It begins with acknowledging the false and unhealthy cure I've adopted in the past. Knowing that I did not always receive the love I needed, I have attempted to compensate by seeking attention. I have tried to be in the popular crowd, and I have cherry-picked my friends. The kind of car I was seen driving, the neighborhood we lived in, the kind of college my kids got into, in retrospect it all seems designed to impress everyone but me. I was looking for attention from important people in the hope that their focus, their friendship, would make me feel important as well.

Yet it is crucial that I do not pass along the same problems to my children. I dare not make insecurity a family heirloom. A sense of inadequacy is the last thing I wish to be a birthright to my own children. From now on, I will instill in them feelings of love and fulfillment and eschew Mafia Love and ceaseless criticism.

As for yourself, it is time once again to contact that inner voice of inspiration and address the void inside you through truthful self-talk:

For me, change starts now. No more criticizing my children, demanding that they get the best grades at all times. Because what are grades really worth in the long run? I want to form my children into fully rounded adults with sterling characters, and there's only one way to do that: I'm going to tell them, simply, that I love them and seek to always inspire them with moral guidance. Unconditionally. And whenever I criticize them, I will preface my critique by letting them know just how much they mean to me. Because that is what I missed out on in my life, and I refuse to let them grow up relying on the same shaky foundations.

Parenting is only one of many areas where attention is deflected away from what's really valuable in life. In particular, our marriages are suffering because people know how to garner attention more than they know how to give and receive love. They don't seem to recognize that marriages should be based on free love.

Yes, I know—thanks to the last few decades of pop- and countercultural influence, "free love" has come to mean commitment-free sex. Something along the lines of open marriages or Erica Jong's zipless . . . Well, let's not quote her directly. But all of these definitions hijack the true meaning of the words. *Free love* actually means just what the words say: love given freely, making the object of affection feel special, beautiful, and secure. We all need to remind ourselves how to feel that way again, and the primary obstacle is our insecure culture's fixation on attention at the expense of love.

What does a marriage based on attention, rather than love, look like? I once knew a couple, Bruce and Ellen, who didn't lack for passion. The two of them were adrenaline junkies, always in search of adventure. The problem was that they fought like cats and dogs.

Week after week, they would battle over which brand of orange juice they should buy, whether they should go to his mother's house for Thanksgiving or hers, which babysitter they preferred. Not a single one of these arguments mattered a bit. The problem was that Bruce and Ellen's relationship was based on friction. They didn't know how to have a healthy, normal relationship based on love, so they drummed up these bickering fights to spark attention, the only emotional experience they seemed to understand. Drama became the lifeblood of the relationship. The more they needled each other, the more attention they received from each other.

People in unloving marriages unwittingly create drama in their relationships to get more attention. We mess up our relationships subconsciously, because we only know how to thrive on discord and mood fluctuations. We invite the hell of marital dysfunction.

To fend off this disease of attention in our relationships, the only cure is a bracing self-talk:

I am starting to see that this volatility, the daily drama I feed off, these arguments, the battles and the skirmishes, day in and day out, have taken the place of real love in my life. In the same way that some adrenaline junkies live from danger to danger, I've become addicted to friction. Marriage is not supposed to be adversarial, and the volatility that my behavior causes every day is terrible for my children. I need to turn away from this insatiable hunger for attention and rebuild my marriage on love.

This isn't the only form that attention-based relationships take. More troubling behaviors arise when the need for attention grows out of control. Certain people are driven to exercise and diet until their bodies change unrecognizably—all to push their partners into expressing approval of their physical appearance. I know some women in their sixties who have had so many face-lifts that their eyes are now on opposite sides of their faces, like ET. It's tragic and it's not pretty, but in their minds that's what they had to do so that their husbands and the rest of the world would still give them attention.

Sometimes couples use quickie sex to garner attention, employing lovemaking not as an expression of intimacy but as a way of getting an instant fix of unhealthy hormonal attention. In all too many cases, spouses can use jealousy as a cudgel against each other, playing out a drama that has nothing to do with real love.

I used to be friendly with a woman named Jessica. Her husband was loving, devoted, and dutiful: he was home on time every night and he never skimped on his responsibilities. Nevertheless, she was hyper-jealous. If he went to buy tickets to a baseball game and cracked a joke with the woman at the counter selling them, Jessica would flip out. One day she confessed to me how tormented she was by this jealousy. She begged me for advice on how she could keep her husband from straying.

I shook my head. "Jessica, you have to recognize the truth here. Your husband is blameless in this situation. In fact, the only person who needs to stop and take stock is you—you need to understand: *your jealousy is an expression of self-loathing*. It's a feeling that you're not worthy of love, so you compete even with the most distant strangers in the most casual interactions. Any momentary attention, however innocent, that your husband gives to another woman makes you feel instantly deprived. Yet you're supposed to feel loved even in those moments when he is giving others attention. And short of the two of you moving into the desert to be completely alone, he's going to have to interact with other people, some of whom will be women.

"You don't feel loved because you feel as if you're not worthy of love, whether because of your upbringing or your experiences in other relationships. And now you've hit on jealousy as the way to sustain your husband's attention. You want a man who cherishes you and appreciates you, and you know what? You've found one. But to keep him, you don't need to play a cop or a CIA agent. You need to be a healthy human being, first and foremost, and tune out the voices of self-loathing and jealousy."

What are the lessons for the rest of us? Interrogate your inner voice of inspiration, and use it to penetrate the truth of your romantic history by saying,

In my relationships I can now see that so much of their substance was based around attention, rather than love. I tried so hard to impress the people I was dating. I laughed at jokes that weren't funny. I offered over-the-top compliments that I didn't mean, all because I thought that I wasn't lovable enough. I was desperate for love, so I settled for attention. And it didn't last.

My marriage can't be based on attention, only on solid, romantic love. I will no longer go on the treadmill or to the gym in the hopes that my spouse will spontaneously congratulate me on trying to look good for him/her. I did not get married to have to earn love. I've already earned it. I am a devoted, hardworking, and sexy spouse. I am adequate. Rather, I'm going to go to the gym to feel healthy and good about myself, which is what makes me beautiful to my spouse in the first place.

From now on, I foreswear having quickie sex with my spouse that is not attentive or passionate. *Quickie sex is a ploy for attention, rather than love.* It's about feeling instantly connected based on hormonal urges alone. It's where something biological, rather than something uniquely human, connects you. And submission to that kind of instant, erotic, attention-grabbing behavior, which wears off just as soon as sexual climax is achieved, has been injurious to our marriage. On the contrary, when we make love, I want it to involve real displays of affection.

Popcorn-style lovemaking is not what I need. Hors d'oeuvres, a fine wine, and a delectable main course is exactly what the

doctor ordered. And that's why I also want us to make love i
dimmed, romantic, preferably candlelit settings. I don't want
sex to be about attention. I want it to be the orchestration of
two personalities, the synthesis of two into one. That's how
I can heal my confusion of love and attention. One bone, one
body, one flesh.

In the end, all of the ways that we confuse love and attention boil
down to filling the void inside us. If we're to relieve our social stress
and improve our marriages and our relationships with our children,
we need to pinpoint our attention-seeking behavior and listen to our
inner voice as it guides us toward the true path of fulfillment and love.

I have to be careful in my own life, believe me. Every year,
Newsweek publishes a list of the fifty most influential rabbis in the
United States. The list was started four years ago, just as I began
working on *Shalom in the Home*. When the list came out, a producer
called me up and said, "Congratulations, you're one of the ten most
influential rabbis in the country." I thought, "Wow, what a compliment." Yet as I thought about it some more, I realized that this had a
really negative side. It didn't make me feel good about myself at all;
it only made me feel insecure. I couldn't help but start to worry, "Am
I going to be on next year's list? Will I go down or up? Who's ahead
of me?" It fostered insecurity.

I'm not alone in this, either. Once you become a number on a list
and are ranked, it may feel good in the short term, but it soon feels
oppressive. Ted Turner has said that the *Forbes* list of the four hundred richest people in the United States actually stops people from
giving to charity. The more they give, the further down they fall on
the list—so why would they ever do something that would diminish
their worth? He proposed an alternative. A list of the four hundred
biggest givers in the country.

In my case, this list of influential clerics makes me feel more insecure. Even though I know better, I can't help but say to myself,

o to stay on the list?" I want to be recognized as real difference, rather than as someone who anking. If you measure your worth by these , you'll find yourself lying awake at night, wondering ur life is worthwhile, whether your relationships are truly ble, and whether you're even worthy of love in the first place.

What can you do to assuage your worries and recommit your life to love, rather than attention?

For so many of us, the solution begins with our parents. So often we bury issues that need to be aired. As a result, we end up not feeling as close to family members as we could be and nursing old wounds all of our lives. Remember, the void that we fill with attention begins early in life, under our parents' tutelage. If we don't address their early failings, which turned us into the people we are, we may lose that chance forever.

I once knew a young woman named Amber whose father left the family when she was eight and didn't speak to or contact her for a decade. Amber had a car accident when she was seventeen, right after she got her license. Her father called her out of the blue while she was in the hospital. He said to her, "This is your father—I heard about your car accident, and I wanted to know how you are." Amber couldn't speak. He kept on asking, "Are you okay?" and she refused to respond. After a while he hung up. When he called back, she wouldn't answer the phone.

Amber later told me that she was never going to talk to him, she was just so angry. She kept asking herself, "How could he have abandoned me?"

I told her, "You're right—his actions are almost unpardonable. But you're never going to have another father. This is it. If he never called you, then okay—obviously, you two would never be able to have a relationship. He would prove himself to be a total deadbeat. But he called you now. To ignore it is simply the wrong thing to do."

People usually think I'm mistaken in this regard, but it's just not healthy to go through life thinking that your father does not love you. Ten years of their relationship were lost, which is terrible. But there are worse outcomes still in the offing, if you don't repair your relationship and, in the appropriate way, confront your parents.

Michael Jackson, with whom I was once very close and for whom I tried to provide inspiration and direction, died at way too young an age because he could not find the love he needed, mostly from his father. From an early age he was told to use his talents to get attention. That attention became a drug that he couldn't live without. Over time he received advice that to sustain the public's interest he should do things to grab attention even if they made him look peculiar. His antics caused people to talk and the tabloids to fixate on him. Yet when he woke up one day and discovered that people no longer found him amusing but instead called him "Wacko Jacko," he felt a pain most of us can scarcely understand. And it was a pain for which he turned to ever-increasing doses of prescription medications until his body buckled under the strain.

Michael was a noble soul who reached for higher things. I always urged him to reunite with his father, to discuss his feeling of being unloved, and to trace the reasons behind why he became the way he was. But Michael didn't feel ready to do that. He and his family paid a terrible price for not resolving that void. We should bring redemption to his life and to his honesty in confessing how badly he sought his father's love by learning from this omission.

I've told you about my father. He and I had an incomplete relationship that dated back to when he and my mother divorced. At age eight, I no longer really believed that he cared that we were leaving, even though he, of course, cared deeply but struggled to show it. It took me years to address this with him. But one day, after I was married with kids, I turned to him and asked, "Abba, tell me one thing: when you struggled to show love and affection all of those years, was it because you couldn't show it or because I didn't deserve it? Was the flaw in you? Or was it in me? I just need to know."

He looked at me in utter silence. By the way he retreated from the question, I knew his answer. There was nothing wrong with me. I wasn't a bad kid. But my father, like many a good man who started life in poverty and had to tread water just to keep his family afloat, felt severely challenged about showing vulnerability. He had been working since the age of ten. He had steeled himself against life in order to survive. Showing emotion meant weakness, and weakness meant perishing.

Honestly, in my heart I already knew that was true, but it meant so much to see him acknowledge it. Our relationship has changed completely, thank God. My father and I are immensely close, and, after my wife, he is the most important adviser in my life.

Say to yourself,

Love is the glue that unites all of the disparate forces of the world together. It's the gravity that pushes everything back to cohere into one. I need that same force in my own life to keep from feeling as if I'm torn in twenty different directions. I need to remind my parents that I love them in spite of their failings and faults, and I need to accept the fact that they love me, too—even if they don't always show it properly.

Starting today, I am going to fix my precious relationship with my parents. I am going to speak to them—respectfully and lovingly—about all of the omissions in our relationship. I did not come into this world to hold things in and build resentment. I want them to know my perception of things. I'm going to tell them that in my childhood I often felt an absence of love, as if they were too busy with other things. Granted, I'm going to make sure that I also acknowledge all of the good, but I'm going to be honest about some of the scars these omissions left.

Even less so do I want a relationship with my parents based on attention, rather than love. The days of my calling them up to tell them about all of my professional achievements are over. I'm not here to show them that in the end I proved myself. These are my parents, for goodness sake. I have nothing to prove to them. Furthermore, I have the right to be loved unconditionally, instead of earning attention by making them proud of me.

It's not the past that matters but the present. Whatever was not done earlier can be done today. And once I've resolved matters with my parents, my life will be a clean slate on which I can sketch an optimistic future with my family—one that is based on love, not on attention.

To develop a personalized relationship with your inner voice of inspiration, ask yourself the following questions. Respond to them, and let the answers guide you on self-talks of your own devising.

Am I obsessed with celebrity culture? Do I lie awake at night, envying the riches, beauty, skills, and success of others?

Do I find myself doing things just to get people's attention, even if my behavior is negative or unhealthy? Do I name-drop and gossip about others?

Is my physical appearance more important to me than my character?

Do I go crazy every time I see a sign that I'm aging or putting on a few pounds?

And what is the effect of all of these behaviors on my children? Do I instill in them a curiosity about the wonders of the world? Do I instruct them to succeed through study and hard work, or are they getting the message that they need to suck up to teachers to secure a passing grade?

Am I a showy person? When I succeed financially, do I run out and buy things to prove to the world that I'm a success? Or do I draw from the lessons of my inner voice of inspiration to live with humility?

3

Give the Ego Its Due

CONVERSATION 3

I will inspire myself to utilize my ambition and make a contribution that is larger than myself.

Wat kind of person are you? Ambitious and driven or calm and imperturbable? If the former, you are following the dictates of the ego. If the latter, you may have learned to deny the ego.

Ego is the source of ambition. It pushes us and drives us, telling us we have to succeed, gain wealth, and make a name for ourselves. The ego is on the constant lookout for recognition. It grants us no rest, as I know all too well. Yet at the same time, ego isn't the force of evil that it's made out to be.

To be sure, we're not meant to be driven by narcissism or selfishness. But neither are we meant to quash the ego.

Runaway best-sellers such as Eckhart Tolle's *A New Earth*, a good book that was heavily promoted by Oprah Winfrey, tell us that the ego gets in the way of our relationships, makes us easily offended, and generally blocks our path to enlightenment. On the surface, this argument makes sense, and the book was one I much enjoyed. According to Tolle, "A genuine relationship is one that is not dominated by the ego." Who among us doesn't have a brittle and easily wounded ego that has caused us to fall out with loved ones or stopped us from living for a noble cause larger than ourselves? How many precious relationships have been lost because our egos were offended or our pride slighted by some petty offense?

Tolle continued, "To create suffering without recognizing it . . . is the essence of unconscious living; this is being totally in the grip of the ego." Also true. How many of us have snuffed out happiness in our own lives because we feel like failures when we measure our achievements compared to those of our friends? And how many of us have not taken necessary risks because of the fear of failure that results directly from an eggshell ego? We're afraid that if we fail, it will be proof positive that we're utterly ordinary.

Yet Tolle and other assailers of the ego frequently take their argument too far. In *A New Earth*, Tolle wrote that "the ego is in its essential nature pathological." Wait a minute. Surely, the ego is not some terrible disease. It's a part of you, part of your makeup. And it can be used for profound good—but only if you give the ego its due.

Let me explain using my own story.

As a man with his own fair share of insecurities, I struggle with ego issues all of the time. I veer from altruism, where I do the right thing and help people without looking for recognition of any kind, to self-centeredness, where I ask, "What's in it for me?" I sometimes feel like a yo-yo, torn between the conflicting angels of my nature.

I am blessed with nine wonderful children, thank God, and they consume an enormous amount of my time, as is proper and to be expected. Would I be more professionally successful if I had more time to work?

Furthermore, as an orthodox rabbi, I have constraints on what I can do professionally. My strict Sabbath observance prevents me from taking advantage of many TV and radio opportunities. Because

I keep kosher, I can't dine with colleagues and use meals to network in the same way that others can. Even my beard has turned into something of a snag for my career. Certain friends who are TV producers tell me, "Can't you trim it? It looks unkempt!" (I tell them it brings out my wild side.) Yet the Bible says you're not supposed to uproot the hairs on your face. So I don't, even if I pay a price. These are my principles, and who am I if I lose them?

When I get to agonizing over these inner conflicts between ego and selflessness, I have gone so far as to tell my wife that I'd like to take a scalpel and cut the ambition right out of me. Maybe that would give me peace. Perhaps I'd be calmer and more satisfied. Maybe I'd stop punishing myself. But if I denied the ego completely, would I still be me?

No. I see the ego the same way that Jewish mysticism has described it, as something akin to an ox. You can hitch nearly anything to it. It can pull any load. Why, if you attach a giant charitable cause to it, it can pull the whole thing. Say you want to cure cancer; the ego, looking to win a Nobel Prize, can help you do it.

Whether the ego is beneficial or destructive comes down to the use to which it is put. You can harness a plow to an ox and guide it to harvest tons of wheat that will feed thousands of people. Yet just as easily, you can let the ox roam around in a china shop and destroy everything in its path.

The human ego is raw energy that needs to be harnessed for good. Ambition is not a four-letter word. It is essential to every human life.

When I confront my own ego issues, I stop and address what's going on in self-talk. You should do the same. Slide your internal radio dial over to the voice of inspiration and say to yourself what is manifestly true:

Ambition has always been a double-edged sword in my life. On the one hand, it's pushed me to succeed. It's made me want to make something of myself.

On the other hand, my ambition has caused me a lot of pain. It's pulled me away from my family, keeping me in the office till late at night so that I could make more money and impress the boss. It's also made me into a jealous person. When good things happen professionally to my friends, I can't help but feel diminished. Gore Vidal perfectly described my feelings when he said, "Whenever a friend succeeds, a little something in me dies." It's not pretty, but it's the truth. Just as my ego brought me achievement and success, it's also brought me these negative feelings.

Many times I've cursed my ambition. It's always pushing me, always making me feel inadequate unless I push further and work harder. Sometimes I feel like packing it all in, giving away all of my possessions, and moving to Africa to work with needy kids. If I were to sacrifice my ego altogether, maybe then I could purge selfishness from my being and subordinate myself to some great cause.

But I also know that such a radical reaction is misguided and extreme. It would be all too easy to pack it in and run away, instead of addressing the issue and elevating my ego. Difficult as it is, I instead should aim for balance. Yes, I aspire to find the golden middle path.

This definition of the ego as something harmful is not a new development. In fact, it's central to Eastern religions such as Buddhism. The Buddha said, "All pain results from expectations unfulfilled." If you kill off your desire, if you subdue the ego, then you will not know any pain. He also said to his followers, "The parts and powers of man must be dissolved; work out your own salvation with diligence." For the Buddha, anything that smacked of ego, ambition, and self-interest of any kind was to be avoided.

It's not hard to see why that kind of attitude is appealing, even today. We in the West are nothing if not ambitious. We want to have the best jobs, to live in the best neighborhoods, to take the most enjoyable vacations. We want to make an impact, and we want to matter. The drive to achieve can wear us out.

To be sure, the ego has caused much depression and unhappiness in our lives. Yet it has also produced an incredibly prosperous society with world-class hospitals, among other amenities. It has created a wealthy government that can take care of its poor and hungry. And it has led to technological innovations in areas such as food production so that none starve.

Compare that to the situation in the Eastern countries that primarily practice Buddhism. Look at nations such as Cambodia, Laos, Tibet, Thailand, Nepal, or Bhutan, where the ego has undergone perennial assault. True, the populace may not have all of the ego ailments that are common in the United States. Statistically, people in these societies are nowhere near as depressed. They are, on the whole, more spiritually enlightened and arguably more content. Their women don't suffer from eating disorders such as anorexia or bulimia. They aren't forced to self-medicate as do people in the United States, who ingest three-quarters of the world's antidepressant opiates.

Notice, however, that they also lack the hospitals, the roads, and the infrastructure that we in the West have built. Their populations are not as well nourished, nor are their governments as stable or secure. Some can barely sustain their own populations, let alone offer foreign aid. They lack our high standard of living. And I'm not talking about wall-to-wall carpeting or plasma TVs. All people deserve to live in dignity, and in many of these countries where the ego is identified as the enemy, there seem to be an excess of slums and people living in crowded and challenged conditions.

Why the disparity? To be sure, there are many causes of poverty that are beyond the scope of our current conversation. But what I am focusing on is the fact that because many Eastern countries don't share the West's passion for a free-market economy that is driven by ego, ambition, and the desire to succeed, those countries have abandoned the benefits that an ego-driven society can accrue. *The ego deserves its due.* If you sacrifice ambition, you'll also lose all of the good things that it can bring—such as achievement, prosperity, and success.

In contradistinction to ancient Buddhism, Judaism has always held a healthy view of the ego. The Talmud relates a story of how the ancient rabbis once pursued the ego (which they termed the "evil inclination") through mountains and rivers. When they finally captured him, they put the ego in a box. Yet just before they were going to kill him, they realized the enormity of what was about to happen. "What should we do?" they asked. "If we kill him, the world will be destroyed." They recognized that if they went through with this, then no man would ever build a house, no man would ever marry a woman. No diseases would be conquered. Nothing would ever move forward. The rabbis agreed merely to blind him (and who would dispute that ambition can be blind at times?), before setting him free once again.

This is an amazing story. There is nothing quite like it to be found elsewhere in any religion. The point, of course, is that there are two sides to the ego. Yes, the ego is selfish, paranoid, materialistic, and jealous. But the ego is also the part of us that fuels ambition, a desire to distinguish ourselves and to provide for our families. The ego provides our sex drive, our desire to connect and be intimate, our need to be known and cherished.

Think about it: have you ever met anyone without an ego? Egoless people have problems at least equal to those of individuals with excessive egos. They cannot be in relationships. They have nothing to offer. They don't believe in themselves. They are riddled with self-doubt. A man who seeks to destroy his ego becomes a bore to his wife. Likewise, a woman with no ego becomes a doormat to her husband. His attraction to her will disappear as she loses her self-assertion and becomes haggard and submissive.

What would happen if all of the doctors in the West transcended their egos? What if they didn't want to live in nice houses or win a Nobel Prize? Would they still be curing disease? And what if we got all of the American capitalists to transcend their egos? What if they no longer wished to own private jets and yachts? Great, they're not as materialistic. More power to the people. But what would happen to all of the jobs they create?

To find your balance, look inside yourself and begin an honest self-talk: "I'm realizing that I *do* have an ego—and that's not something to be ashamed of. There is nothing bad in wanting to make something of my life. My ego tells me that I'm not ordinary, that I'm special. It wants me to share my gift with rest of the world. That doesn't sound like an out-of-control ego, one that is dominated by narcissism and self-absorption. In fact, it's not a bad thing for me to seek to support my family and buy them nice things. Only if I become overly materialistic, living only to earn money and buy things to impress other people—only then will my relationship with the ego have gone wrong. No, instead I will pursue a more moderate path."

The Bible tells two stories about the creation of humans. The first chapter of Genesis says that man was created by God "in His image." He was created majestic and distinguished, the master of his domain, the arbiter of his own destiny. He was also immediately created with a woman. He knew neither loneliness nor any sense of abandonment.

The second chapter of Genesis, however, tells a very different story. Man was created from "the dust of the earth." He was created forlorn and solitary, with no female companion. The very first emotion he experienced was loneliness. Later, God will take a rib from this second Adam and enclose it in flesh and bring forth Eve. The commandment God gives this second Adam, unlike as with the first, is not to master the world and subdue its inhabitants but to tend to the Garden of Eden and protect it.

These two stories reflect two different human experiences. The first Adam is, in the words of Rabbi Joseph Soloveitchik, majestic man. This is the part of us humans that is ego-driven, defined by ambition and the desire to make a mark on the world and subject the elements to human control. But lest his ego get out of control, there is a second facet to this Adam. His double, Adam II, represents the humble and vulnerable side of our nature.

In finding balance between the two sides of our existence—self-absorption and self-abnegation, promotion of self and subordination of ego—we become whole. The coexistence of the two Adams enables humanity to achieve a healthy equilibrium between ego-assertion and ego-denial, between putting ourselves forward to make our mark and knowing when to retreat to allow others to coexist in the empty space. To subdue our nature to the point where we are only the second Adam would be terrible for the world. Nature would never have been improved on, and we might all still be living in mud huts. Yet the flip side of having out-of-control egos that think the world exists solely for our benefit is what led to an environmental crisis in the first place. We cut down all of the trees and polluted the rivers in an effort to make nature useful to us. Balance is achieved by embracing both sides of the disparate Adams.

> *Man's ego shouldn't be quashed, but neither*
> *can it exist untamed.*

Use the voice of inspiration to motivate yourself to find that balance. Say to yourself,

Egotism and egolessness are everywhere. I see extremes in so many of my friends. Some of them have given into ego completely. They drive themselves with no end in sight. They're always traveling, always working, never at home. I see them in a fancy new car nearly every year. They seem to enjoy their possessions more than they do their friends. That is, if I can still call them "friends," because I notice that a lot of these ego-driven friends tend to trade up when it comes to friendships. One minute you're their friend, and the next they've dumped you in favor of more important people. They treat people as if they were commodities, to be used and discarded, and I never want to act that way.

Then there is the other extreme, my friends who are not ambitious at all. They're simply not motivated to do anything but live lives filled with endless, meaningless distractions. They don't try to improve themselves by reading books. To the extent that they have something to say, it's usually clichéd. It's not that

I'm looking down at other people. It's rather that I know life is precious, and it's a sin to squander our potential.

So I'm going to give the ego its due. I will listen to the part of me that wants me to be more and that believes I was created for higher things. I'm going to channel my ego into a definition and a pursuit of success that are truly healthy and special. Yes, I want to be a somebody, but a somebody is not a person who has a lot of money. It's someone who is wise and in control of his/her passions. It's someone who is a hero to his/her children and whose spouse looks up to him/her as a noble person. It's someone who retreats from conflicts and is available to people in need.

Find the balance between affirmation and denial, self-promotion and self-sacrifice, ego-gratification and ego-abnegation. It's the only way to master the power, inspiration, and ambition of the ego and use them for your own purposes. As we shall see, in no area is this truer than with human relationships.

I counsel many parents, and I am, of course, a parent myself. Perhaps it is something about the culture of parenting today, or maybe it is due to the prevalence of self-help gurus—but whatever it is, the mistakes I most frequently witness parents making these days involve the total loss of ego. Parents honestly seem to believe that they have no right to tell their kids what to do.

I once counseled a family with a fifteen-year-old daughter named Michelle who was having sex with her boyfriend.

When I spoke to Michelle's parents, Donna and Steven, I strongly recommended that they break up the relationship. "Sex is for adults. She is your responsibility. And you must lay down the law. She is not allowed to have sex at such an early age," I said. "Stop thinking that you're her friend. You're her parents."

They looked back at me as if I had just walked out of the Stone Age. "She's a young adult," Donna said. "We can give her our opinion, and we did. We don't think she should be having sex either. But it's her decision." Here was a girl who could not legally drive a car or buy a beer. Yet she was mature enough in their estimation to engage in an activity that brought a roller coaster of emotions that could affect her for life.

I'll never forget another egoless parent whom I once knew. Sarah was happily married with two children. One day her husband had a heart attack and passed away at the age of forty-two. Devastated, Sarah was left the widowed mother of a twelve-year-old daughter, Tanya, and a son who was ten.

Four years later, Sarah had become unhealthily dependent on her children's love. By now, Tanya was sixteen years old and dating really nasty guys, much older than she was. It was perfectly obvious to any observer that she was looking for a father figure.

When Sarah told me about the things Tanya was doing, I was alarmed. She thought nothing of coming home with her boyfriends and making out with them right in front of her younger brother as he watched TV. It was unacceptable, and I told Sarah so—but she protested, "She's a young adult. I have no right to tell her what to do. She's old enough to decide these things for herself." (Notice, once again, that term *young adult*, which embodies something of a contradiction. After all, are you an adult or not? And by what criteria do we distinguish between a young adult and a big kid?)

No matter what I said, I couldn't convince Sarah to change course and reactivate her ego. She let her daughter walk all over her, and by the time Tanya was eighteen, she was engaged to a man fifteen years her senior. She got married, had her first child a few months later, and after three years, she finally left the man after suffering verbal and even physical abuse.

Sadly, to this day Tanya refuses to speak to Sarah. She completely blames her mother for not stopping her from ruining her life. What she's effectively saying is, "Where were you? You were my mother, and I was a confused sixteen-year-old girl. Why didn't you stop me from doing this to myself?!"

So, if you're a permissive parent, a hands-off, complacent, or laissez-faire mom or dad, take a good look at the consequences of what you're doing. Look at Michelle, the sexually active fifteen-year-old, and Tanya, a divorced mother at twenty-one, and imagine the same fate for *your* children. Then change your approach by admitting what needs to be done. Say to yourself,

I see exactly what's happening. I'm failing to give the ego its due, and the ramifications for my children may be dire.

I recognize that I am crippling my children because I'm not assertive, because I am egoless. I understand now that the choices I make today—or, rather, the choices I *fail* to make—have a tremendous impact on my children's future. Far from thanking me for being weak, my kids will one day hold me accountable for abrogating my responsibility to provide firm moral guidance. That's why it's time to stop dithering and assert my ego.

That isn't the only problem that parents have with the ego. It isn't always a matter of a broken or weak ego—sometimes we just get lazy and prefer to let life pass us by as we sit in front of the television. Rather than being unable to assert ourselves, most of us can hardly be bothered to care to do so. We don't want to admit it, but if we really look at our behavior and ourselves, we'll see that our hearts don't seem to be in parenting. It's just so much work!

If the stress of your day leaves you drained when it's time for you to interact with your kids, the solution is, again, a deep and bracing self-talk. Admit the problem and take the first step toward solving it. Speak the truth and say,

I never wanted to be a lazy parent. But when I come home tired from work, I'm emotionally spent. The temptation to veg out in front of the TV is great, and my children demand so much time, effort, and hands-on activity. It's just tough to muster up the energy.

But an absentee parent, dozing on the couch? That's not who I want to be. I realize that life is short. You blink, and your kids will have already grown up. I don't want to miss that.

My ego can be my engine, but only if I constantly draw on it and use it. I want to summon the energy to do homework with my children every night. I hated math when I was in school. I hate it even more now. But I aspire to be a great parent, so it's time to buckle down and get involved.

I want to be one of those parents who never misses reading their children bedtime stories, who can point to an entire library of books they've read to their kids over the years. As my kids grow older, I want to be a source of wisdom and advice to them. And if I give the ego its due, I'll be well on my way.

One of our generation's most insidious plagues is the midlife crisis. We all know someone who has experienced one of these—if we haven't gone through one ourselves. (I've had about five already.)

It's all too easy to fall prey to a midlife crisis: its victims once dreamed and aspired to certain lofty goals. They were going to *be* somebody. Maybe they were going to invent some great new technology or write a groundbreaking novel—maybe they were going to make a billion dollars or become world famous. But now, at forty-five, they are working dead-end jobs, living in modest houses, and nowhere near achieving what they thought they would.

Their dreams weren't exactly realistic, nor were they healthy. Much of what they envisioned was shallow and superficial, dictated by what popular culture defines as success even if it didn't mesh with their unique talents or gifts. But the solution was not for them to have their egos crushed.

Instead, people need to use this situation to inspire themselves to greater heights. When a man wakes up at forty-five years of age and feels as if he has done nothing with his life because he doesn't own a yacht, instead of feeling sorry for himself, he should be redirecting his ego gratification into something truly meaning-ful and worthwhile—such as getting more involved in his children's upbringing, mentoring youth, volunteering for a great cause, or exploring a new career that fit his deepest passions. This is a much better alternative than the even shallower ego gratification of get-ting a Porsche and a blonde.

A midlife crisis occurs when we have a warped understanding of our value. It often starts when we compare ourselves to people our age and what they've achieved. Most men fall victim to the feeling that they're still struggling financially. Because it comes from com-paring external qualities, there's no end to it—there's always someone richer. Even a man as wealthy as Warren Buffett can feel as if he's a failure—"I'm not the richest man in the world," he'll think. "I'm only the second richest." Then a guy like Bill Gates may get to thinking, "I may be the richest man in the world today, but adjusted for inflation, John D. Rockefeller was far richer than I am." That's why defining yourself by ephemeral, external qualities can be so dangerous.

I once counseled a man named Arthur. An accountant at a small firm, he looked around when he was forty and found that all of his friends were wealthy, while he was only "comfortable." He'd made enough money, sure, but compared to what some of his peers were making, it was a drop in the bucket. His ego was sorely wounded. He told me he was a loser, a failure. "I feel as if I have no direction in life," he said.

Like so many other men in midlife crises, Arthur looked for another way to redefine his self-worth, and he found it in a female colleague. He started getting close to a woman in his office—an attractive younger woman who made him feel good about himself. The voice in his head would tell him, "You're a nobody—why'd you ever become an accountant, anyway?" She'd counteract it by telling him what a great guy he was—special, smart, attentive.

They started to have an affair. When Arthur's wife found out, she was surprisingly forgiving. She said to him, "I'm not going to leave you. I understand you're going through a difficult time, and I want our marriage to survive this. All you have to do is get rid of her—have her fired, cut off relations with her, and never see her again. Then we can rebuild our marriage."

But Arthur couldn't give the woman up. He procrastinated and complained—what would she do without her job? How would she find one elsewhere? She wasn't a bad person and he wouldn't throw her to the curb.

I said to Arthur, "The saddest thing I see is that you honestly believe you're making a choice between two possible partners. You think you're deciding between a wife who isn't as compelling as she once was and a younger woman who is beautiful, unattached, and completely convinced of your greatness. You're treating them as if they were comparable choices. Yet you're deciding between something real and an illusion!

"On one hand, you have a real life and real kids, and you're a real success. You have a wife who loves you so much that she's prepared to forgive you. On the other hand is a woman who hasn't had your kids, hasn't nursed you through sickness, hasn't stuck by you when you've caused her indescribable pain. You're choosing between air and fantasy. Arthur, choose the real deal!" Yet his ego couldn't let him see the truth.

If you want a good example of an ego gone out of control, look at Mel Gibson. A man who makes a movie retelling the world's oldest lie—that the Jews killed Christ—has got serious prejudices. I said years ago that I had no doubt he would expose himself in time as both a bigot and a man with serious anger issues. Sure enough, we now have the drunken anti-Semitic tirades, taped threats against his girlfriend, and racist rants to demonstrate his true character.

What Mel Gibson did is really not so different from what Arthur did. Gibson dumped his wife of twenty-eight years to move in with his Russian girlfriend, Oksana Grigorieva. He, too, discovered that his imagined choice of a devoted wife versus a new girlfriend was an illusion. There never were two people to choose from. As soon as things got bad, what did Grigorieva do? She taped his conversations, made them public, and destroyed his life. Of course, who could blame her, as it seems she was subjected to scary and threatening domestic violence from a seemingly unstable person. Yet Gibson's wife, who suffered through all of his narcissism, cheating, and everything else, kept her silence and remained loyal and dignified. If she was married to an abusive husband, then she would get rid of him quietly rather than bring the whole world into her family's life. Mel Gibson foolishly thought there was a choice. There was no choice at all. He spurned a real relationship and went with an illusion instead, and in the process, he ruined himself.

Don't let this happen to you. Don't let your damaged ego force you into making false choices or destroying the relationships that are most important to you. A midlife crisis is simply the expression of an ego out of sync with the realities of the world. Instead, give the ego its due, and let its power motivate you not to strive for meaningless external achievements but to make the best of life's most important values.

Speak to yourself, urgently and sincerely:

I have to admit, my greatest fear is the fear of failure. I have run from that fear my whole life, and it has propelled me to work hard and succeed. There's no shame in wanting to be a success. But I don't want to be propelled by my insecurities or by fruitless comparisons with my peers. Rather, I want to be motivated by my potential. My ego tells me that I have unlimited potential locked inside of me. It is my obligation to maximize that potential and make the most of my life.

I have an obligation to make the most of my professional life. I have to overcome the fear of risk-taking. I don't want to be foolhardy, and I have to always be cautious. But great rewards come specifically to those who are prepared to take risks. And I'm tired of being held back.

Yet I would be remiss if I didn't aspire to be the world's greatest spouse as well. If any kind of success is important, that should be the true measure of my ambition and success. Ego can be insatiable if I define myself by how much money I have in the bank or by my position at work. But it can be my greatest asset if I use it to power my way through life and to become a truly formidable spouse, parent, and human being.

The truth is that the ego will always demand its due. It will, in the final analysis, require its pound of flesh, whether we give it willingly or not. It cannot be forever suppressed.

The religious person who believes he is abnegating his will utterly to God often finds his ego manifesting in his condemnation of those whom he declares to be less pious than he. The wife who allows herself to be a doormat to her husband's wishes will end up decrying women who are more liberated as selfish feminists too self-absorbed to put their families first. The broken man or woman who gives up on his or her dreams will end up being profoundly jealous of others who are more successful than they. And the poor, oppressed masses living under the tyranny of a dictatorship will end up hating the people of the free West for their materialism and egotism and will declare them the very enemies of humanity and decency, as we have witnessed all too painfully, especially through contemporary events

There are clear limits to what you can achieve while denying the ego. Even Barack Obama, in his acceptance speech for the Nobel Peace Prize, admitted that he couldn't embrace only Martin Luther King Jr.'s example. Nonviolence and passivity can work in a democracy, but what do you do, for instance, in a place such as Tibet? There are few people I respect more than the Dalai Lama. A warm, unquestionably great and righteous man, he has never in his life resorted to violence—he's a true inspiration to the world. On the other hand, there's an ineffective side to his denial of the ego. The Tibetan people have lived under tyranny for more than fifty years now. Where is the inspiration to fight for independence, the ambition and drive to struggle against totalitarianism?

At the first hint of even nonviolent resistance, China comes in and decimates everyone, as we witnessed with Tiananmen Square.

The ego has motivated so much good in history. It's foolhardy not to draw on its formidable powers. For a leader such as George Washington, ego was vital. In *His Excellency: George Washington*, the historian Joseph Ellis described just how much self-cultivation Washington understood. He wanted so badly to impress powerful people—and he groomed himself for years to be equal to the task at hand.

What really differentiated Washington from his peers was that he knew how to control his ego. After rising to power so triumphantly, he voluntarily gave it up. At the end of the Revolutionary War, Washington went to the Maryland state capital and resigned his commission as commander in chief of the Continental Army. I took my kids twice to the room where he resigned his commission in Annapolis, Maryland, just to bask in the atmosphere of so noble an act. His nemesis King George III inquired about what Washington planned to do next—and when he learned that Washington intended to return to his farm, the king remarked, "If he does that, he will be the greatest man in the world." Like Moses, who conferred his powers on Joshua, or Cincinnatus, the Roman general who in 458 BCE served as dictator to save the republic against invasion but quickly retired to his farm as soon as the danger was removed, there had never been an example of someone so in control of his own ego that he gave up power and returned it to the people. No wonder Washington was the man who ushered the United States into existence—his control of ego was absolutely representative of the combination of power and deliberation, of checks and balances that has long defined this nation. Washington knew what many others do not, which is that the ego has a place—but that there is also a time to defy it, channeling your ambition into causes larger than yourself.

In the end, the ego will always find a way to express itself. It can be a healthy expression: the ambition to contribute one's gift to the world. It can be a violent, long-suppressed outburst: a popular uprising that overturns a dictator and frees a suffering people. It can even be an unhealthy, unsustainable spiral: a midlife crisis that leaves its victim insatiable for more money, success, status, or even sex.

Yet if you subordinate the ego to a cause higher than yourself, it can be your engine. By giving the ego its due, it can help you achieve lofty goals.

So let your voice of inspiration give you a newfound honesty about the ego. Tell yourself,

It's taken some time, but I've now figured it all out. I can and will use my ego to help push me to greatness. It means using my God-given talents to make my own personal contribution, based on my unique gifts and talents, to others and to the causes that mean something to me.

I can't be utterly submissive—that's unfair to my ego and an unhealthy way to live. So I refuse to abase myself. Self-help gurus shouldn't make me feel like an evil person just because I have goals and ambition—they're part of what makes me what I am. Likewise, my religion shouldn't make me feel as if I'm nothing but chaff before God—I want religion to make me feel like a spiritual giant. My existence was called forth by God for a grand spiritual purpose. He empowered me with Herculean strength and the motivation to make something of my life in order to get the job done. I even have a right, indeed a moral obligation, to challenge God, to thunder against the heavens, in the face of seeming divine miscarriages of justice. That's what the word *Israel* means: "He who wrestles with God."

I'm here to achieve and contribute, and the ego is but one of my tools. With its help, I'm going make good on all of my ambitions: to be the world's greatest spouse, the world's most attentive parent, and a true inspiration to my community. My life, my family, and the world around me will be the better for my contribution—and it's all because I know to give the ego its due.

To develop a personalized relationship with your inner voice of inspiration, ask yourself the following questions. Respond to them, and let the answers guide you on self-talks of your own devising.

Do I ridicule those who are more ambitious than I am? Do I always find fault with people who commit themselves to achieving great things?

Do I recoil when I hear news of others' good fortune—even my dearest friends'?

Am I making the most of my life or, with the aid of my ego and my inner voice of inspiration, could I be more motivated, more inspired, more ambitious?

Do I use my money to do good? Do I provide wealth for my family? Do I improve the world with my presence, every day that I am alive?

4

Defy Death

CONVERSATION 4

I will remind myself that I can live forever
through the impact I make on lives that follow me.

How many times have you made it home from a tough day at work and wanted nothing more than to kill a little time in front of the television or on the Internet? If your spouse or your children try to engage you in conversation, you shrug them off, claiming you've earned some time alone. Yet in a flash, a few minutes become a few hours. You've wasted the evening on drivel, and your family has gone to bed, leaving you with the anemic company of a flat-screen TV.

Wiling our lives away in front of a TV or on the Internet has become de rigueur in America. We work so hard that we forget our most basic human needs. The long hours turn us into robots, and when we finally make it home, we've expended all of our energy, leaving little for our families. We choose distraction instead of connection, fabricated entertainment rather than real company, and we allow our spirits to shrink as we consume up to five hours of junk per night, seven days a week, turning our brains into cabbage and our hearts into plastic.

It doesn't end there. In this culture, our day-to-day lives are just something to be waited out and suffered through on the way to retirement. We pat ourselves on the backs as our 401(k) accounts swell, deferring all of our hopes and dreams until later in life. When inevitably we get bored or depressed along the way, we smooth out our true feelings by taking pills, further deadening ourselves. With the extra money we kill ourselves to earn, we take vacations where we lie on the beach like a bunch of corpses, forsaking vacations that can lead to adventure—such as camping trips and hikes—for holidays that lead to nothing.

If you want to live a better life, cultivate better relationships, and raise better children, it's not enough to jump-start your ego: you've got to resist the urge toward distraction and numbness. *You have to defy the culture of death.*

I know what you're saying to yourself—a culture of death? Hold on, isn't that a little extreme? Look at the situation I just described: when you empty your brain of all thoughts, watching insipid television shows, acting like a zombie in front of the computer, are you really alive? Or are you immersing yourself in oblivion and numbness, states of consciousness that are only a few degrees separated from lights out?

Yes, I understand the need to forget one's problems and pressures for a while. I, too, like watching the occasional TV show and movie. But what happens when fantasy begins to supplant reality, when the death-embrace of TV unwinds families, when an addiction to Facebook supplants interactions with real human faces?

How much of your life do you waste succumbing to distraction?

The only way to get your answer is through self-talk. Ask yourself,

How much time do I spend in front of the TV? More hours than I can count. And I've gotten *so* addicted to the Internet. Sure, Facebook is great—it lets me check up on my friends and stay in touch. But at what price? Compulsively checking it takes so much of my time.

I can't even control my texting any more. My fingers just move on their own. I'll be in middle of meetings or out to dinner with friends when I'll abruptly realize that I'm only partly there. I've been texting the entire time. I don't want to fool myself about my ability to multitask anymore. Not even a genius such as Albert Einstein could concentrate fully on two things at one time, let alone three or four. My electronic addiction is truly becoming all-consuming.

What do I really feel when I'm watching reality TV or when I'm clicking refresh on my Facebook wall? Nothing! It's all so mind-numbing. Does it matter what status messages my high school classmates are posting? Will the outcome of *American Idol* really determine anything about my future? And it's not the watching that is problematic. Rather, it's my obsession. If one of my kids dares to speak during one of my favorite shows—and they all seem like favorites these days—I find myself shushing them in harsh terms.

I have to admit the truth: my life is becoming increasingly consumed by numbness and distraction. *I recognize that I am moving toward a culture of time wasting and death.*

It's time to make a change.

Death doesn't merely ensnare us by pulling us away from reality and life; it also looms at the end of life. That's why it's impossible to fight the culture of death without reimagining how we live and die.

Some years ago, I attended a lecture by Rabbi Manis Friedman about the terminally ill. He said that after years of counseling the elderly and those with terminal diseases, he had found that once doctors told them that their days were numbered, at that moment their lives effectively ended. Rabbi Friedman insisted that it was his responsibility as a counselor to defy this trend, to do everything in his power to ensure that hope didn't perish. Even with a terminal illness, he said, people should still cling to life with all of their strength. They dare never give up hope. Even as we prepare for death, we must be attuned to life.

When I first heard this, I was confused. Is it really right to lie to yourself about the reality of death? Don't you have to at least say good-bye to everyone once you know that your time is short? Yet once I started to counsel the terminally ill, too, I saw that Rabbi Friedman was absolutely right.

Sure, you can say to yourself, "There's a good chance I've only got six months to live—I'd better start tending to my affairs." Fair enough. But for those six months, you still have to *live*. You have to inspire yourself to infuse every moment with meaning. Indeed, some of the people I know who had only a few months to live did so with a zest and vitality that would put the rest of us to shame. The best-known recent example of this, of course, was Randy Pausch, who, less than a year before his untimely death, wrote his moving book *The Last Lecture* about making the most of life.

The Talmud tells a story of a Roman nobleman who came to see one of the great rabbis. The Roman said to the rabbi, "I don't understand—when God created Adam and Eve, he knew he'd have to punish them. He *knew* that the flood would come and destroy everything. So why did he even bother in the first place?"

The rabbi mused and then said, "Do you have children?"

"Yes," the Roman said, "I do have children, and I love them."

The rabbi said, "Well, before you had them, didn't you realize that they were going to die?"

The Roman was taken aback. "Well, yes, but I was more concerned with the fact that I would raise them, give them an education, and someday bounce their children on my knee."

The rabbi said triumphantly, "It's just the same with God! He focused on the good, on the celebrations that people were going to experience even if He was aware that life might not have the happiest ending."

This is exactly why I believe that the Dr. Kevorkians of this world, those who would end life early, are deeply misguided. Live life as if you're going to live forever. Be present. And if death catches up to you, then at least you'll go down fighting.

I'm not saying we shouldn't prepare for death, but prepare for it while holding your nose. I have car insurance, but I don't drive thinking that I'm about to get into an accident, God forbid. I believe people are supposed to live as if they will never die.

"But, Shmuley," you might say, "don't be ridiculous. A car crash isn't inevitable, but death is." My response is—really? Who says? When Professor Christiaan Barnard, the celebrated surgeon who performed the world's first heart transplant, lectured for me at Oxford University in the midnineties, I asked him what he was working on next. "Mankind's oldest disease," he said. "Old age."

Okay, look, I haven't taken leave of my senses (at least, not completely). I realize that we're all *probably* going to die. And I'm not suggesting that you get cryogenically frozen like Walt Disney or Ted Williams. But neither should you be fixated on death. Death is not part of your life. It's outside your control. Yet it's in your power to try to prevent it as much as possible. Embrace life.

Those two words, "Embrace life," compose the command Moses gave to the Israelites on the last day of his life. They beckon to us thousands of years later. Let's say you have a close friend with whom you've had a falling-out. You can either choose death—stubbornness, an inability to apologize—and watch the relationship die, or you can pick up the phone and choose life. "Hi, I miss you. I can't believe we were once so close and we're now so distant. I hope you'll forgive me, for I want us to be friends again."

Maybe you have a marriage that is going south. You can choose death—"My spouse is impossible, and I want a divorce"—or you can choose life. You can come to your husband or wife and say, "I love you. You're my one and only soul mate. And I know we can make this work." Choose life.

Perhaps you have a teenage child from whom you're becoming more distant every day. The teen barely speaks to you, always preferring the company of his or her friends. You can choose death and let your child drift away. Or you can choose the life of the relationship. "Son, it pains me that we're not as close as we used to be. I have some complaints, and no doubt you have some, too. From my side, I want you to know that you are the most precious thing in the world to me. I am sorry for anything I did or didn't do. Tell me what I can do to make things better. I will. I promise. I'm really listening now." Yes, we're all capable of always choosing life.

Ask yourself, "What am I?" Your voice of inspiration will supply the one and only answer: *"I am life!"* Practice this self-talk:

Life is God's most precious gift. A single moment of life is more precious than an eternity of death.

Life is all that is blessed. Death is the dark void that swallows all blessings, the absence of the spring of life. This is why life is so precious.

I have to maximize my life, for time is so short and there is much to do! I mustn't spend my whole life reading other people's Facebook updates, because what's the point of prolonging my life, exercising, and eating healthy, if I'm only going to squander my potential by obsessing over other people's lives? Why bother going on vacation, if I'm just going to lie around like a corpse and have minimal interaction with my kids? No, I'm going to take my kids on adventures. We'll follow the Lewis and Clark Trail. We'll camp at the national parks. We'll see the great Civil War battlefields such as Gettysburg and Vicksburg. I'm going to take them white-water rafting and sea-kayaking. I'll condition my children to appreciate not tourist traps with silly trinkets and mini-golf but the true beauties of nature. For nature is life, and I want my children to love life, live life, and protect life.

And I'm going to reinvest myself in the deeper aspects of my relationships, transcending the merely functional and zeroing in on the intimate. For what's the point of being married if there's no love?

All life is precious, and I resolve to embrace it, starting now.

. . .

I mention marriage and parenting because they especially have been touched by the culture of death. Think about how wrong it is that the creation of new life, of your own children, succumbs to the same culture of goal-oriented numbness and death.

For parents, it often takes the form of pessimism. We take kids with learning disabilities and put them in special education classes, transforming them into "special needs" children. One of our children was diagnosed with a reading disability. His teachers put him in a special education class. His performance suffered even more as soon as he started attending the new class. We couldn't avoid the fact that he needed help. After we pulled him from the special education class, we got him a shadow, someone to be in the regular class with him and assist him when he needed it. In that situation, he flourished. He has since been in and out of special education classes. I am not knocking their necessity, but only as long as their purpose is to transition the child, however slowly, into a regular, mainstream class.

I know parents of a three-year-old child with Down syndrome who are fighting for their child to be in a mainstream class, accompanied by a helper. They believe that their child, with proper assistance, can lead a largely normal life. They've taken on an entire school system to get it done. And what if they end up being proved wrong? At least they wrestled, they struggled, and they affirmed life. They demonstrated that their child is just as alive as any other child. At least they did not capitulate without a fight.

Even if we're not being outright pessimistic, our expectations for our children remain dangerously low. Look how many teenagers today come across as zoned-out, tech-obsessed zombies. The real world doesn't engage them. They are cold to real people and real communication. Only when immersed as cyber warriors in increasingly violent video games do they come fully alive. But once the PlayStation is turned off, they struggle to show basic emotions.

It shouldn't be this way. America has prospered because it is a profoundly life-affirming culture. It became the richest nation on earth because of its citizens' industriousness and nonstop hard work. No challenge was too great, no horizon too distant. Every great civilization before America succumbed to the "inevitability" of historical decline. Yet we in America know that as long as we learn from our mistakes and continually renew our values and our energies, our civilization can go on forever, with God's blessing.

Death can be defeated.
Decline is not inevitable.

It would be a tremendous shame to squander the American future by letting our children languish, fall behind in school, and become technology-obsessed robots. Allowing the culture of death to overtake our nation's promise would be the greatest tragedy of all.

We must take action, and the precursor to action is a truthful self-talk. Say to yourself,

I am wondering about the true state of my relationship with my children. Do we speak to one another regularly, engaged and curious about what the other has to say? Or is my relationship with my children, like much else in my life, half dead?

I've always wanted to be the kind of parent who would come home and enliven his/her children. I remember when the kids were younger, and I'd walk into the house and they'd yell, "Daddy's home!" "I missed you, Mom!" Today, they're sitting in front of their computers or listening to their iPods, and they barely know I'm alive. They don't come to me with their problems. They don't ask for advice.

I want to be a living presence in their lives—and I'm not content simply to be the ATM who doles out allowances and gas money.

So I'm going to bring my relationship with my teenage kids back from the dead. Every night we'll take part in a family activity that requires us to connect. I'll break the silence that has reigned for so long between us. We're going to talk. We'll study something together every night: lessons from the Bible, current events, historical parallels. Or else we'll just have a discussion—a legitimate conversation, our first in a long time.

I know that it's going to be tough at first, but after the initial rough parts we'll all feel more alive. There's no other choice. The stakes are too high to let the culture of death prevail over my family.

The strange thing about our society is that if you look to most religions for help in evading the death culture, you'll come away disappointed, for the culture of death has unquestionable theological underpinnings.

Many religions treat life as if it were nothing but an antechamber for heaven. Death is when the soul is finally liberated from the cage of the body. Christianity believes that death represents an individual's release from the darkness of this world to bask in God's radiant light. That's why many Christians have a wake. Death becomes a celebration. Notice that Christians call the day of Jesus's crucifixion *Good* Friday. It's good because Jesus, through his death, redeemed mankind from sin. Someone had to die, someone had to suffer, in order for redemption to come about. Death is the key to life. Buddhism asks you to disconnect from the world—even from your own self—to achieve nirvana.

Some world religions go so far as to glorify death. We've seen this most strikingly in extremist Islam, where men and women invite death, both their own and that of their innocent victims. We've seen press coverage of mothers who cheer when they discover that their teenage sons have blown themselves up, remarking that they wish their other sons would do the same thing. These people have been led to believe that death is superior to life, that only in heaven will they be rewarded.

Many rabbis make the mistake of preaching that suffering is redemptive and that death is a release. I have penned countless articles refuting this destructive idea. Suffering scars, rather than redeems. And there is nothing blessed about death.

The religion that I grew up in, Judaism, is a celebration of life. Our dead are buried far outside the city walls because we refuse to glorify death or have it exist in the midst of life. Jewish dietary laws prevent us from eating milk and meat together because milk is the elixir of life, while meat is death. We don't make love during menstruation because, although the purpose of sex is intimacy rather than procreation, menstruation still represents the lost opportunity for life. Particulars aside, everyone can take cues from Judaism's reverence for life—even if they're not Jewish.

Eric and Kelly came to me for counseling not long ago. The two of them were evangelical Christians who had been married for years. Eric was a classic workaholic who barely spoke to his wife and kids, vegging out in front of the television instead. Kelly had been twenty when she married Eric, and now she felt as if her entire marriage had been nothing but a funeral. She wanted to live, but the culture of death and numbness had swallowed up her husband.

I sat them down and said to Eric, "Let's talk seriously about what you think of your life. Do you find your faith to be exciting or boring?"

He thought about it for a second and then shrugged. "Boring," he said. His job? "Very boring." I asked him about his wife next. He looked directly at her and said, "Kind of boring." Clearly, this guy was in serious trouble.

"How about your kids, Eric?" I asked.

He smiled at this question. "My kids are always interesting. They're the best part of my life."

"Look," I said. "There's a very beautiful verse in the book of Deuteronomy, in which Moses speaks directly to the Jewish people. He gives the Torah to them and tells them that it will make the nations of the world sing. And here's the important part—'Know,' he said, 'it is not something empty from you.' What it means is that if you ever feel that religion or, for that matter, your life or your marriage *isn't* electrifying, edifying, and elevating, you can't blame it on God, you can't blame it on life, and you can't blame your spouse. Rather, the emptiness, the boredom, is coming from you. I've been a marriage counselor for twenty years. In that time I've learned that there are no boring people and no boring human stories. So if you find the world around you, your religion, and your wife boring, *the boredom is coming from you.*"

Hearing this, Eric went silent. His wife, Kelly, immediately spoke up. "He's right," she said, looking Eric squarely in the eyes. "If you continue to act this way, do you think the kids will want to be around you, once they're old enough to see the truth? They won't want to waste their time with someone who is so dead to life—they'll do everything they can to get away from you!"

The jury's still out on Eric. So far, he hasn't improved. I'd be dishonest if I told you that every story has a happy ending. But his story can still be illuminating, if only by giving you inspiration to avoid the culture of death, numbness, and boredom that he still embraces. Consult with your inner voice of inspiration and ask yourself, "*Why am I wasting my life? Life is such a precious gift. Every second of it. So why do I waste so much time? What's my excuse for not living life to the fullest?*"

I think you'll find that the answer to that question will never be good enough. Because you're tired? Because you worked a long, hard day? Because, like Eric, you're "kind of bored" with your life? Remember what Moses said, and remember that this emptiness not only comes from you—it's up to you, and only you, to reject it.

So during your self-talk, be clear and say,

My life is nothing but a measure of time. When people ask me how old I am, that's what they mean. How many years have you *been*? How long have you walked this earth? Every moment is precious. Every experience is something I can learn from, even the painful ones.

I have to make the most of it, and in order to do that, *I resolve to defy death.* I have to value time and not waste it. I have to ensure that every year that I live, I progress, I move forward, I become wiser, I grow. I'm not a stone that sits in stillness, nor am I a tree that is stationary. I am a human being. I live, I grow, I prosper.

To stave off the culture of death, we need to follow the examples of heroes who have done it before us. There is no such thing as a great man or woman who has not defied death. Some have summoned intense courage to carry on with important endeavors despite the threat of annihilation.

Martin Luther King Jr. knew that people wanted to kill him. The night before he died, he mentioned the possibility of his death during one of the greatest speeches in modern American history, the mountaintop speech, delivered on April 3, 1968, at the Mason Temple in Memphis. King spoke of a recent assassination attempt and then alluded to the many death threats that were flowing in. "Well, I don't know what will happen now. We've got some difficult days ahead. . . . Like anybody, I would like to live a long life. Longevity has its place. But I'm not concerned about that now." He was prophetic: the very next day he would be shot and killed by James Earl Ray on his own hotel balcony.

Yet the fear of death didn't stop King from believing that he was born to lead and born to contribute. "Let us rise up tonight with a greater readiness. Let us stand with a greater determination. And let us move on in these powerful days, these days of challenge to make America what it ought to be. We have an opportunity to make America a better nation. And I want to thank God, once more, for allowing me to be here with you." He believed that America was a great country that could overcome its horrible history of slavery, racism, and discrimination. He knew others would benefit from his life. He also knew that even if he were killed, his dream would live on. He might not make it to the promised land, but America would. "I just want to do God's will. And He's allowed me to go up to the mountain. And I've looked over. And I've seen the promised land.

I may not get there with you. But I want you to know tonight, that we, as a people, will get to the promised land."

In a very strong sense he is still alive. In Judaism, a person is said to be alive if he or she still affects the living, still leaves a trace on the cultural, religious, and political environment. Martin Luther King Jr.'s memory continues to inspire and affect the nation, just as in the days when he marched from Selma to Montgomery.

The *New York Times* recently published the story of Brendan Marrocco, a veteran of the war in Iraq who returned home after an IED left him without arms or legs. Yet he refused to give in to death. He fought to survive and then struggled to live a fulfilling, adventurous life, even with a damaged body. The two wars in the Middle East have produced countless heroes such as this one, who returned home from the cauldron of death only partly alive. Yet they have taught the rest of us how to live our lives to the fullest.

I often look to my own mother's example for inspiration. She never had it easy. By the age of twenty-three she had five children. She did everything herself: cooking, cleaning, and dealing with the stress of having very little money. She and my father were divorced when my mother was only thirty-two, and then she was alone for decades until she finally met a man who treats her, thank God, with love and respect. Yet through all of this, she never soured on life and she utterly rejected any negativity or pessimism.

At my wedding in Australia, she stopped me as I walked toward the chuppa, the Jewish wedding canopy, and said, "Shmuley, remember all of those fairy tales you read when you were a little kid, how they all ended in 'happily ever after'? Well, they don't have to be fairy tales. You can make them real. You can live a life that is happily ever after. If you fight with your wife, apologize. If you ever hurt her feelings, make it up to her. Be a good man, and be a good husband." I was amazed to hear these beautiful words from a woman whose marriage had been so unhappy.

I've taken them to heart. All the time, I tell myself, "Forget about death—I want to live a life that is happily ever after. And the best way to achieve that is by devoting myself to being a good man and a good husband." I've never regretted it.

So let your voice of inspiration motivate you to enumerate the ways that you will defy death and change your life:

First, I'm going to make sure that I take advantage of my brief time here. I'm going to find more energy. I will start doing an hour of exercise every day. I'll push myself, even when I don't feel like it. Physical activity is a must. Those who are alive are animated and mobile, while those who are dead remain stationary. Even when my heart is dull, I still have the ability to make myself feel.

Speaking of my heart, I'm going to bring it, too, back from the dead. Every day I read in the newspaper of terrible human suffering all over the world, but I do nothing about it. I sigh when I read that three hundred thousand Haitians died in an earthquake or that people are losing their livelihood because of a catastrophic oil spill in the Gulf of Mexico. Every day I read how brave American troops die in Afghanistan, but I do nothing for the memories of their families. I have allowed my heart to be dead to other people's suffering and to focus only on my own vital interests.

But I want to start feeling again. And it's so easy. I'll begin by gathering up all of the items in my house that are in good condition but that I never use and bring them to charities that distribute to people in disaster areas. Next, I'll start making a monthly calculation of all of our income so that I can give 10 percent to charity.

I will find one charity that really means something to me and will get involved. A nearby organization enlists volunteers to work with mentally challenged children, and I would feel so alive being necessary to these special kids. I'm no longer going to utter empty platitudes about supporting the troops; I'll do something about it—volunteer for the USO, send a care package to a soldier in Afghanistan, or donate time and money to soldiers' needy families. How can I be idle when so many could use my help?

Getting death out of my system also means ceasing to eat all of the foods that are bad for me. The sugary drinks that my kids are addicted to will be replaced with simple tap water. We'll get used to drinking something healthy even if it takes a little time. It's a part of my responsibility to my children to raise them healthfully so that they avoid the culture of death.

Finally, I want to start being happier. The ultimate form of living death is depression. To be depressed is not to feel down. Rather, it's not to feel at all. *I want to feel.* I want to be fully alive. When I'm depressed, I become stubborn and set in my ways. I can't find the motivation to change or be better.

But change is in my grasp. I'm going to stop being a complainer. As the author Dennis Prager says, a bad mood is immoral because of the pain it inflicts on others. No more excuses—I recognize that happiness is a choice, much like the breakfast cereal I have in the morning. I will choose happiness, and I will choose life.

I have a loving family, and I refuse to waste our precious time. Together, we will treat life with renewed excitement and curiosity. My children will regard life as an adventure, and my spouse and I will have new subjects to discuss. Talking about the neighbors or some silly celebrity gossip just won't cut it anymore. We're better than that. We're not boring people who grapple for any subject to fill the emptiness in their lives.

When I'm happy, I feel full of energy and full of life. Every obstacle in my path is so easily overcome. Mountains become molehills. Tiny setbacks are rendered utterly insignificant. I was born to climb mountains and to surmount hurdles. I'm alive, and I'm grateful. And I'll continue to choose life and defy death.

· · ·

To develop a personalized relationship with your inner voice of inspiration, ask yourself the following questions. Respond to them, and let the answers guide you on self-talks of your own devising.

Am I the same person I was twenty years ago?

When I look back at what has changed in the intervening years, can I honestly say that I am making progress? Have I made myself into a better person who is more alive and the wiser for it, or has my heart become calcified?

Have I allowed my intelligence to languish? Has my marriage become starved of affection? Is my curiosity drowning in a sea of distractions?

Am I completely alive, or do I recognize that I have allowed my vitality to ebb? If I have let my vitality slip, what can my voice of inspiration do to help me recover it?

PART II

The Voice of Conscience

5

Do Your Way
Back to Feeling

CONVERSATION 5

I will learn to change my life by substituting
rock-solid action for flighty emotion.

In my career as a counselor, the question I am most often asked
is whether people can change. My own straw poll suggests that
a majority are doubtful, if not outright pessimistic, that change can
ever happen. Small changes are within reach, sure, but when it comes
to life's larger issues, just about everyone seems to doubt that shifting course is possible. I always think of the warning doled out by
armchair psychologists about marriage: don't go in thinking you're
going to change the other person. True change must be pretty rare,
if you believe this.

Yet virtually every inspiring story in world history concerns someone who made a difficult change. Lyndon B. Johnson was a Southern

racist and a supporter of segregation. Yet as president, he signed into law the most significant civil rights legislation ever, the Voting Rights Act. In a speech to a joint session of Congress, Johnson even quoted the famous civil rights march proclamation: "We shall overcome." George Washington was a colonel in His Majesty's army who fought vigilantly against the French on behalf of the British. Yet in only twenty years, he became the biggest rebel against the British crown on earth. If people were incapable of change, history would never progress—we'd be stuck in the past forever.

So, can people change? *Of course they can.* If we didn't believe that, life would not be worth living. Believing that change is impossible is the biggest cop-out of all—it shields us from having to do the hard work of making things better.

Even people who are capable of the most difficult, most historic changes can falter, however. Eleanor Roosevelt was one of the greatest and most heroic women of the twentieth century. She grew up amid wealth and privilege. We have since learned that she was prejudiced as a young woman and frequently wrote casually anti-Semitic letters. Yet with the onset of the Great Depression, she changed. As first lady, she used her position to become a fierce and influential advocate for workers, for the poor, and for civil rights. She even conquered her early anti-Semitism and aided Holocaust refugees and the founders of the state of Israel.

Eleanor Roosevelt's deeply felt compassion was central to her work, but her feelings also prevented her from making changes in her personal life. Before her husband, Franklin D. Roosevelt, was even elected president, she discovered love letters between him and his social secretary, Lucy Mercer. Eleanor was utterly crushed by his affair. Just as her passion for social justice led her to help the poor, her impassioned feelings of betrayal got the better of her. She never forgave him. A marriage between two great human beings was shattered—all because Eleanor couldn't master her feelings and make a change.

I'm not trying to blame the victim. Clearly, her husband behaved reprehensibly. But from all accounts it seems that he wished to make amends, but by then Eleanor had closed her heart. Many women would feel the same. They would agree that a man who engages in that level of betrayal should never be pardoned. Yet the difference here is that she continued to love her husband deeply for the rest of her life. She simply could not forgive him.

Think about changes that you've tried to make in your own life. Consider your failures, small and large, and then, through self-talk, speak to your inner voice of conscience, which like a compass will steer you in the right direction. Ask yourself,

How many times have I promised myself that I would exercise for an hour daily? Call my friend with whom I had a falling-out so that I could apologize? Or stop switching on the television when I should be cracking open a book instead?

How many times have I failed? How often have I promised myself that I would never scream around the children? Yet I continued and never changed a thing, despite all of my promises. I wanted to change—or at least I wanted to want to change—yet change never seemed to happen. *What have I been doing wrong?*

So here it is, the answer to the eternal riddle. The secret of how people can change and become who they really want to be. You *can* change. You just have to know how and remind yourself that we go about it the wrong way completely.

You have to do your way back to feeling.

No doubt, you're wondering what this means.

For most of us, change is all about feelings. We want to be washed away by some powerful, positive emotion that pushes us to want to change, as if we're not strong enough to do it alone.

The husband who has been unfaithful to his wife is rarely proud of it. He'll think, "Sure, I wish I could change. But how can I manage it without something pushing me along? If only I could feel that incredible love for my wife again, if only I felt an overwhelming attraction to her, then maybe I would commit. But until then, what's driving me to do things differently?" When these feelings never show up, he continues to misbehave, idly wondering when change will happen on its own. The answer, of course, is never—as long as he fails to take control of his own future, he'll remain a slave to his basest impulses.

The woman who rarely gives to charity may be a pious person who believes in helping others, but every time she passes a homeless person on the street, the quarters in her purse seem too dear. In honest conversation with herself, she'd say, "I *wish* I could be moved by the plight of the poor. I want so badly to be generous. But my son wants new games for his Xbox, my daughter has been complaining about needing new clothes, and besides, we've been saving up for a Caribbean vacation. Shouldn't I *feel* generosity before I act on it?"

How about the man who makes a New Year's resolution to lose weight and get healthy? On January 2, he'll look in the mirror and say, "Sure, I want to look and feel better. But just thinking about hitting the gym makes me lethargic. I'm looking within myself to find a desire to put in some time on an exercise bike, but it's just not there. On the contrary, I hate exercise, period!" So he throws in the towel, continues to gain weight, and suffers long-term consequences as a result—all because he didn't *feel* like making the change.

The conventional wisdom is that your feelings should come first. Your heart will guide your hands. Your feelings of compassion toward a homeless person on the street will inspire you to give him a dollar. Your feelings of remorse for yelling at your mother will inspire you to call her to apologize. I couldn't disagree more.

Whenever you peer within yourself, seeking out the feeling to try to make a change, you should recognize that a bit more effort is in order. Look deeper. Tune out the whining voice of laziness and the protestations of selfishness and inertia.

Find your inner voice of conscience and let it speak clearly:

My heart does not and should not control my actions. I'm in pain, I feel lousy, and I'm tired. I want to give up or at least wait for my feelings to inspire me with new motivation. But I'm not going to give in.

I'm here to speak to my heart. I'm here to speak to my "I," the essential I, my quintessential self, and the part of me that is not ephemeral. My message is simple: *I control my heart, not the other way around.* I'm going to do exactly what I mean to do. It may hurt, and it will surely be difficult at first, but I'm going to do it anyway.

As the Kabbalah says, "Nothing stands before human will." I promise myself, I'm going to make this change, whether my feelings want to or not.

These aren't mere words—I've experienced the truth of this method myself.

As a boy, I lived in a house with a great deal of conflict. If I had an argument with someone else, I tended to respond by licking my wounds and feeling hurt. I did not apologize. Why should I, when I felt as though I was in the right? Instead, I would sink into myself and sulk.

When I was about fourteen, an uncle took me out one evening to attend a communal lecture. When we got home, he pulled the car up in front of my house and turned the motor off. He told me that from now on, if I hurt or shouted at anyone, I had to learn to say "I'm sorry." "It doesn't matter whether you feel like it or not," he said. "What you *feel* doesn't matter. It's what's right that matters. And if you hurt someone, you have to apologize."

I didn't know whether I could do it. You have to be pretty strong to say you're sorry, but I felt weak. A few days went by, and then he saw me getting into a shouting match with another family member. "Go and say you're sorry," he told me.

"I can't," I said. "They were wrong. I'm the victim here." I had been wronged. The other person had picked on me. "Why should I be the one to say I'm sorry?"

"It doesn't matter," he said. "Even if it's their fault, you're the one who screamed. They may have started it, but you finished it. So go and apologize."

I pushed myself hard. It wasn't easy. Everything inside me was screaming that the other person owed *me* an apology, but my uncle wouldn't relent until I did as he said. So I went to the other room, gritted my teeth, and said I was sorry. A few days later there was another fight, and again my uncle pushed me to be contrite. I went with my head bowed and offered a forced and insincere apology. Then there was a third incident and a fourth. Each and every time I said I was sorry, even when I felt as if I were the one who deserved an apology.

And then something happened. I began to notice that I was starting to feel the apologies after all. With every new apology, I felt as if the argument was over—and that made me feel good. I felt that every time I apologized, I was becoming a better person. I was proud that I had the courage to end the argument. I felt joy at the fact that I could reconnect with people I loved, rather than experience the miserable feeling of harboring a grudge. I felt more mature and in control of my life.

My uncle's intervention has always stood me in good stead. There is still a lot of volatility in me. I wish I were always in control of my actions. Sometimes I lose control in spite of myself. Yet one thing I nearly always do when I argue with someone, especially my wife, is apologize. I return to the scene of the argument almost immediately, usually within about fifteen minutes, and tell her that I'm sorry. My wife does everything for me and is the finest person I know. If we argue, it's usually my fault.

Save yourself the time that most people waste by waiting to feel like changing. Instead, admit to yourself the truth in self-talk:

> Here I am, already an adult. So many of the great things I thought would happen to me have yet to occur. I'm not the person I want to be. I'm angrier than I want to be. I find myself becoming bitter about much that goes on in my life. I bear grudges when I should really let go. I should be so much more positive, but I am not yet the master of my own heart. From now on, it's going to be different.

This will not be like all of those other times when I said things were going to change and nothing happened. That was my fault because one day I felt like changing, and I thought the feeling would last. But the next day that feeling went away, and I was back to square one.

This time I know the difference. *I will not be controlled by emotions; rather, I will learn to be their master.*

Action, action, action. That is my new mantra. In the wake of those hard-fought actions, the emotions are sure to materialize.

The days of my life passing me by are over. I know I'm not going to change everything in one day. But I will start doing the things I know I have to do, even if I don't feel like it. *I will be the master, rather than the prisoner, of my emotions.*

There's no limit to what you can accomplish by doing your way back to feeling. Start by doing your way back to a healthier life. You've heard me talk in previous chapters about eschewing comfort food and avoiding a sedentary life of vegging out in front of the TV. In our society, it seems that overeating and lack of exercise are almost unsolvable problems—yet when I've counseled people on these issues, this method has been instrumental in helping them make real changes.

Marjorie came in for counseling because she felt as if her husband was no longer attracted to her. She had recently put on weight after giving birth and had started to believe that she had lost her looks altogether. Almost unprompted, at the beginning of our session, she turned to her husband and said, "You know, I don't blame you for not being attracted to me anymore. When I look at the mirror, I don't find myself attractive either." Uh-oh. These kinds of statements are instant red flags—such self-loathing is totally unproductive and, frankly, dangerous to relationships.

I immediately said, "Look, Marjorie, you really have to be careful with saying such things. It's neither true nor healthy to say that you find yourself ugly. We all have our imperfections, but beauty is there even so. If you don't behold your own beauty, nobody else will.

"If you want to be thin," I said, "it has to be for a better reason than merely to become more attractive. For instance, it can be very good to lose weight for reasons of health and to improve your willpower.

"You simply have to tune in to your inner voice. Tell yourself, *'I won't allow my craving for food to dominate my actions.'* Whenever you feel a craving, tell yourself not to listen. Say it out loud, if that's what it takes, *'I won't listen to that voice—I'm tuning out that frequency.'*"

It sounds simple, right? It worked for Marjorie, and I would give anyone the same advice, because it's absolutely true. It even worked for me.

I've recently become serious about cycling. I'm no Lance Armstrong, and it's not looking like I'll win the Tour de France (but give me a couple of years), but even so, cycling is a really positive change I've made in my life.

I have always been an active person. I hate to sit still and I love adventure. I especially enjoyed taking my bike to beautiful places and riding along leisurely paths, on flat surfaces, and on the short routes of a novice. Whenever my kids and I would get to a hill, we'd walk the bikes up. Either that or we'd bike downhill and have my wife pick us up at the bottom.

One day I turned around and said to myself, *"This is ridiculous! If I'm going to enjoy cycling, I need to get into it all the way, hills, mountains, and everything else."* Feeling like doing this didn't come first—in fact, I had to fight my feelings the whole way. As soon as I tried to change the difficulty of the rides I was taking, I immediately heard a voice telling me to throw in the towel. About ten minutes up the first steep hill, my legs stopped cooperating, and I felt pain in my knees. Yet at that moment, my memory flashed back to a quote that the U.S. Marine Corps prints on T-shirts—PAIN IS WEAKNESS LEAVING THE BODY. This is absolutely true. I strengthened my will and thought, *"This is not about what I feel.* If I agonize about what I'm feeling, then I'll never do or change anything. *I have to just get to it and commit!"*

Sure enough, once you ride up a mountain for the first time, you realize that even though it's a big deal, you can still do it. A twenty-five-mile ride sounds like a lot—until the first time you try it. It's surprising just how fast the change happens.

Whenever your endurance is giving out, no matter what you're doing, use self-talk to remind yourself of what's really important:

> Tired as I am, as much as my muscles hurt, I know that the only thing protesting is my feelings. Those feelings may say that I should stop what I'm doing, lie down on the couch, and laze the day away. But now I know the truth: *My feelings won't rule my life, as long as I take control.*

It's so easy to become complacent. When you let your feelings control your actions, you end up never pushing yourself. Without even knowing it, you miss out on important parts of your life. It's crucial to fight inertia and to remind yourself to interact with others in a healthy way—even if you don't feel like it at first. That's why you have to do your way back to feeling, not only by exercising and eating right but in your social life as well.

Many of my female friends are success-oriented, ambitious women. They have worked their guts out to get ahead in their careers—but in the process have neglected romantic relationships or even dating. Now that they're reaping the rewards of their hard work, it's time to share these with other people. Yet these intensely motivated people can barely convince themselves to start dating again.

My friend Joelle is a good example. A makeup artist working in television, she's thirty-five, very funny, and attractive. I once said to her, "Joelle, you have so much to offer. You should get out there and meet someone. You should be sharing your life with someone and not just focusing your energies during the day on work."

She didn't agree. "Come on, Shmuley," she said. "There are no good guys out there. I work long hours. I come home tired. Dating is just not worth the effort. Yes, I'd like to be with a guy. But short of Mr. Perfect falling out of the sky into my living room, I can't be bothered."

This kind of frustration is all too common. How is Joelle's disinterest in exerting herself to date any different from Marjorie's inability to lose weight or my own reluctance to ride uphill? It may feel like a chore, but you know that it's the right thing to do. All you need to do is act, and your heart will follow.

I'm sure some of my readers are like Joelle, and my message to you is, *Ignore your feelings—tune out the voice of inertia.*

Say to yourself, in serious self-talk,

I have a lot to share with someone else. I have a special heart, great wit, and deep insights into life. All of this I should be sharing with someone who appreciates me. *Yet my problem is that I have grown cynical.* My heart has hardened. I just don't feel up to love these days. My failure to combat that cynicism is due to waiting around to be swept off my feet, to be overwhelmed by a tidal wave of love. I now understand that it doesn't work that way.

Love is an emotion built of action. I have to *do* in order to *feel.*

I'm going to change. I won't allow my negative emotions to rule my life. I will start going out, even when I don't feel like it. I'll go to community lectures and charity events where a really good person may be waiting to meet me. I know that it won't be easy, and if I don't meet someone the first few times, I'll probably feel pangs of despair. It's so much easier to go home, switch on the TV, and snuggle up under the blankets. But I'm going to resist that urge and do what I know I have to do.

I certainly don't feel like telling people that I want to meet someone or signing up on a respectable Internet relationship site. It makes me feel desperate. But I'm going to do it anyway, because I have nothing to be ashamed of. I'll push myself to do it even when I don't feel like it. And once I do it, I know the feelings will come.

Once I start to act, *my heart*
will begin to thaw.

What situation in human life mixes up action and feelings more than marriage does? So many of us wait for our hearts to change before we alter our actions, especially with regard to how we behave around our spouses. The result? A complacent stasis in which nothing ever changes.

Fred and Celia came to me for marital counseling—and, boy, did they need it. Fred had been neglectful for years, making Celia feel ordinary and boring. As a result, she'd become angry and cold toward him.

Fred claimed that he neglected his wife because of her negativity. Celia argued, in turn, that she had become cynical after years of being ignored. She said she was once a happy young woman, but that she became morose after she married the most selfish man on earth. He said that she had always been a grouch and pushed him away with her meanness.

I told them it didn't matter whose fault it was. "It's not important whether you started it or your wife did, unless you are judging who is right. You have to decide: do you want to be right, or do you want to be married?

"Here's how to make things better for a change. Fred, your task is to give your wife three compliments every day. They can be for her looks, what's she's wearing, something nice she did for you, or the great mom she is.

"Celia, you have to say three positive things to your husband each day. Thank him for how hard he works to support the family, what a loving father he is. You can reminiscence about a special time you spent together in the past."

They both protested at having to say things they might not mean.

I shook my head. "Don't you guys get it? Sure, when you start, it will feel unnatural, even artificial. But as you go through the process, it'll begin to feel authentic. It will slowly become sincere. And the reason is that it's actually not contrived at all. You have a beautiful wife, Fred, but you're utterly distracted. If you focus because you're forced to offer a compliment, you'll see what you've been missing all of this time. The same applies to you, Celia. You can't blame your husband for making you negative. *No one can make us become something we don't want to be.* You're choosing to be negative. But you can become joyous again—and the method is by *acting* joyous. By not only focusing on the positive but by also enunciating the positive. The more you say it, the more you'll feel it and ultimately become it."

As Celia and Fred changed their behavior, their feelings followed suit. They had some rough times, and they still fight. Yet in general, they found themselves appreciating each other anew.

What does a man say in deep self-talk about his marriage? He must let the voice of conscience be his guide and admit, "I've always wanted to be a romantic husband, the kind of man who wakes up in the morning and tells his wife how beautiful she looks. I have never respected people who just take others' kindnesses for granted. But I have to be honest. *I fear I am becoming complacent.*"

A woman may have an entirely different conversation with herself: "I've always wanted to be the kind of woman who was soothing to her husband. I know it's tough being a man, always agonizing over the family's finances and how the bills will be paid. But I react poorly to my husband's neglect. He's not the only one working for the family—I feel utterly unappreciated. And yet I have never wanted these feelings of bitterness and unhappiness to define me. I want to have and to be a soul mate, not an antagonist."

Both husband and wife can improve their lives, their happiness, and their marriage by *doing their way back to feeling.* Say to yourself, "I know that I should get into bed at night and give my spouse a massage. Even just two nights a week, I know he/she would love it if I massaged and caressed him/her. I may not feel like it, but from now on, I am going to act first, and let my feelings change later."

One problem I often encounter in marital counseling is a husband who is a selfish lover. On average, married couples have sex once a week for five to seven minutes. The reason: the husband focuses on his own sexual pleasure, leaving his wife unsatisfied. It's a natural male impulse, and it has to be resisted. And it can be, by the husband *doing* his way to feeling.

Force yourself, despite your natural impulse to climax, to be patient. Start by kissing your wife. Then fondle and genuinely cherish her body. No doubt, the impulse to jump straight into coitus will be present, but resist it. You are not a man controlled by his emotions. You are the master of your feelings. Resist the impulse. Be a gentleman.

Next, give your wife a long massage, focusing first on her extremities and then moving slowly to her erogenous zones. Again, the impulse for coitus will rear its head. Ignore it. Do your way to feeling. Learn to enjoy seeing your wife's sexual response. Feel the deep pleasure of watching the woman you love come alive as a sexual being, with you as the stimulus. Then focus on bringing her to climax, garnering great personal satisfaction from the pleasure you're giving her. Slowly, it will happen. Habit will become second nature. What begins as something you do will end up being something you are. You will become a great, patient, gentlemanly husband who makes his wife feel amazing. In regularly bringing her to climax, you will purge her of all of the built-up tension from working and raising kids that so many wives and moms carry with them. You will help her rise above the daily grind. And she will love you for it, all because you became one of those unique men who *does* his way to feeling.

Say to yourself,

I'm going to start every morning by telling my spouse something loving. I'll begin my day with appreciation. That's what I want to be—a grateful, loving partner—so that is how I will act.

I'll push myself to become a better parent, spouse, lover, and human being. The method? Doing what needs to be done, and letting my feelings follow. Because sure enough, they will.

All of this sounds pretty hard, doesn't it? Forcing yourself to do things you don't feel like doing may *seem* almost impossible—until you try it. Yet it really is the secret of success. If you command yourself over and over again to change, tune out the voices that tell you to surrender, and get that inner voice of conscience humming, you'll find that the change you seek will soon become second nature.

The first couple of times you try this, sure, it will prove challenging. You'll feel a lack of energy and the same selfish urges that push you to neglect your spouse, veg out in front of the TV, exchange quantity time with your kids for that overused concept "quality time," overindulge in comfort food, and leave the family to their own devices. Yet once you force yourself to resist those urges, to *do* even though you don't *feel*, within a matter of days the feelings will come. You'll be thrilled to see your wife's face light up as you compliment her before you leave for work. You'll feel like a hero as your kids open up to you at the dinner table and tell you about the teachers they love and those they loathe. TV will pale in comparison. On nights where you don't read your kids a bedtime story because you're forced to stay late at work, you'll feel a void. You'll miss the feelings that you've grown used to. And finally, that intimate, physical connection with your wife will feel more potent and pleasurable than ever, making the TV fade to secondary importance.

One summer I had two books to complete (look, I've got nine kids to feed) on top of my normal busy schedule. I did not think I had any time to spare for a family getaway. My wife told me that we were taking the kids on a long drive into Canada. Period. It was their time, and I wasn't going to take it from them. So we went. My wife did most of the driving, and I wrote on the road. It was hard. The kids were loud. I was tired. But when it was over, ten days later,

I was truly sad that it was ending. In the days that followed, I missed being around my children 24/7. I felt lonely without them. They're the best, and I was so glad that I had the privilege of their company every minute. And yes, this is the book I wrote a large chunk of on the road.

Take control of your life. If you really want to change, then you cannot wait for your emotions. Doing so only makes you into a victim. Rather, you have to start by doing it, whether or not you feel it. Push yourself to do whatever you want to change into. At first, it will be hard. The second and third times will still be challenging. Yet after those first three times, everything will fall into place. The change will be slowly burned into your character, transforming from something you do into something you are.

Find your authentic inner voice of conscience on your internal radio dial. Avoid the other childish, selfish, and base voices that would persuade you to act against your interests. Envision the person you want to become, then *act*.

Tell yourself,

I'm going to pick up reading again. I used to love books, and I can fall in love with them all over again. I want to know more about history and current events. I want to be more spiritual. I want to refamiliarize myself with the Bible. I'm going to read more spiritual books that teach me to be content with my life, more satisfied materially, and hungrier spiritually. I'm going to sit in synagogue/church even if I feel bored. I'll force myself to delve deeper into the service. I'll ask the rabbi/pastor about the deeper meaning of his sermon and try to apply it to my life. I'll do all of this even if I don't feel like it, confident that if I do it right and regularly, the feelings will come.

Defy your feelings. Engage in actions that will gradually change your heart, and let your emotions catch up to you. Just think about it: if your charitable giving depends on how you feel at any given moment, then you won't end up being very charitable. A lot of the time you'll look at someone sitting on the street as a beggar who ought to get a job. You work—why doesn't he? Instead, let the following self-talk smooth over your feelings of resistance:

I know the kind of person I want to be, and stingy isn't it. Ten percent of everything I earn does not belong to me. I want to start giving more to charity. I'm going to set up a charitable account into which I immediately put 10 percent of all of my earnings. I'll find causes that do good work and need my help, and I'll give them money regularly. I'll be charitable with my time as well. I'm going to volunteer two hours a week with these organizations. I'll take my kids with me so that they will learn to be selfless. It will make them better, happier, more balanced adults.

I don't want to be a selfish person. I don't want to be someone who spends only on himself and his family and who prioritizes buying a dumb new electronic toy while others have nothing to eat. I know that the more I give, the more I'll feel. *My heart will follow my hands.*

The same is true of being a better son or daughter and friend. You know that your parents did everything for you, but you're busy. You've got your own family now. Nevertheless, do your way back to feeling. Tell yourself,

From now on, I'll call my parents more often and schedule more visits. I'll do the same with my grandparents. I know that how I treat my elders is how my kids will eventually treat me, and I want to be an extraordinary example to my children.

I know I've allowed tension to develop between me and my brothers and sisters. Petty sibling rivalries have unwoven the natural bonds of affection that used to connect us so strongly. But I'm going to do and be better. I'll call them and apologize for any insensitivity I've shown or wounds that I've caused. I know it won't be easy. I fear that they will not accept my apology. Yet I know that being a good person is not about what we accomplish but about what we do. And I'm going to do the right thing.

There's no end to what you can change when you do your way back to feeling. Simply find a vision of greatness that is within reach, tune out the voices telling you that it's impossible, and act. Say this out loud:

I will find a cause to work for so that my life amounts to something more than just self-interest. To be sure, my family is the most important cause of all, but as a family, I want us to be devoted to something. I'm going to find an organization we believe in, a charity to which I can contribute, or a church we can all help with our hard work.

This is no passing fad. Mine is not an emotional attachment. It is a conviction that will slowly, with my commitment and effort, become eternal and everlasting. As the master of my emotions, I can accomplish anything, and by and by, I will become the person I always hoped to be.

To develop a personalized relationship with your inner voice of conscience, ask yourself the following questions. Respond to them, and let the answers guide you on self-talks of your own devising.

Am I the person I truly want to be? Or does my voice of conscience reveal areas where I can improve?

How good am I at enacting change? When I say I'm going to do something, do I actually follow through?

When my spouse is offended by something I've said or neglected to do, am I ready with an apology, or do I sit and stew, waiting until I feel like changing?

When I get my paycheck after a couple of weeks of hard work, do I immediately think of the new clothes I need and run to the mall, or do I also think of a charitable cause I would like to support and send a check so that the needy benefit?

Is my voice of conscience helping me see the way to action? Can I confidently say that my actions inform my emotions, or am I still a slave to my feelings?

6

See Yourself
in the Third Person

CONVERSATION 6

Holding my life in the palm of my hand, I will become translucent.

I spend my days endeavoring to be a healer, a doctor not of the body but of the heart. People come to me for advice, recounting tales of their painful childhoods, broken marriages, out-of-control children, and squandered potential. I listen to their stories and offer counsel as best I can. I started doing this when I was twenty-two years old, and after more than twenty years' experience I have discovered something important: *the only people who truly heal are those who become self-aware.*

Self-awareness these days is the rarest of things. As I've discussed in previous chapters, most people seek their identity only in externalities. From TV to music to the Internet, we constantly absorb external stimuli, never peering within ourselves for self-knowledge.

Instead, our culture tells us who we are, what we should wear, how we should think, what we should own, and how we should love.

This wasn't always the case. Not more than two generations ago, writing was the principal form of communication for absolutely everyone, with the sole exception being speaking. People kept diaries that revealed their innermost thoughts on a daily basis. They wrote long letters to their friends expressing insights about themselves and the world they lived in. Writing was a tool all people could use to turn themselves inside out, discover what made them tick, and become self-aware. It was the best and most widely available way to see themselves in the third person.

Nowadays people text one another and write e-mails that are as brief as possible—sometimes they are barely even grammatical. That's wonderful if you want to get a lot done quickly but terrible if you hope to gain personal insight. Indeed, without a mastery of language we cannot fully understand ourselves. We simply lack the necessary tools.

When we do look at ourselves, we are all too easily stopped in our tracks by defense mechanisms and excuses. This is something I see all the time: it seems no one can apologize without including a "but." If a man breaks a glass, he might say, "I apologize for being careless—*but* why does my wife have to keep such fragile objects all over the place?" If a woman is being overly negative, she might apologize for lashing out but then accuse her husband of drawing her into a fight. *We can rarely accept our own culpability in our actions.*

Frankly, it's scary just how little we know about our own motivations. And if we don't know why we do things, how can we possibly heal ourselves when we do something wrong?

However out of vogue it is in the modern world, open and unencumbered self-awareness is the key to human development and change. For a good example of its power, we can look back to the biblical figure of Joseph. His many brothers reviled him from an early age. They sensed his powers and were jealous that their father, Jacob, showed him favoritism, so when he was still just a boy, they threw him into a pit and sold him into slavery. They told their father that Joseph was dead.

Yet despite these dire circumstances, Joseph rose to prominence in Egypt. The reason? His incredible insight. He had a talent for interpreting dreams, and by using his skills, he managed to win both Pharaoh's favor and a position of supreme power in Egypt. By the time he had become viceroy of Egypt, he could easily have crushed his brothers, who were themselves starving and searching for food across the land. A lesser man would have gone ahead and taken vengeance—after all, it was their hateful actions that almost sentenced him to a short, miserable life as a slave. But Joseph was well aware of his unhealthy, baser impulses. He recognized them for what they were, and what did he do in response? He defied his own very human desire for revenge.

He decided to orchestrate an elaborate display to test his brothers and their fidelity to their half brother, Benjamin. All along, he was keenly aware of the human capacity for revenge, to hold a grudge after being slighted. Nevertheless, he worked consciously against it. It's truly impressive. This self-awareness can give people incredible abilities, for it allows them to master their own emotions.

Another great example of self-awareness in action is Abraham Lincoln. As Doris Kearns Goodwin has shown in her book *Team of Rivals: The Political Genius of Abraham Lincoln*, Lincoln came to power over a divided nation. His election was contentious, and plenty of people would have loved to see him fail.

Like any person, Lincoln wanted to establish himself and succeed in the eyes of his peers. What set him apart was his self-awareness and insight. He was able to bypass his defense mechanisms and deeply understand his own craving to be recognized. He was so knowledgeable, in fact, that he innately knew how to accommodate that need in others. He placed in his own cabinet a group of men whom he very well knew would disagree with him and with one another—his famous "team of rivals"—but through his superior insight and magnanimous dealings with each member of the group, he was able to forge compromises and ultimately rescue the United States from division and disintegration.

We can't all be like Joseph or Lincoln in our everyday lives. Self-awareness isn't easy, and it's hard to see past our defense mechanisms.

The truth is, America is a society whose citizens are challenged with personal problems, from divorce and broken families to low self-worth, drug and alcohol addiction, and depression. All of this amid a gazillion self-help books and an untold number of TV and radio shows supposedly devoted to helping us fix our relationships. Yet we still haven't healed ourselves because we think that healing involves remedying an issue.

> *Real healing is not about solving a problem:*
> *instead, it is about becoming self-aware.*

Humans are not, nor will they ever be, perfect. Rather, healing involves learning to struggle to be better by identifying the inner forces that we have to combat. Even if we cannot gain complete mastery over every impulse, we can still identify our motivations. Knowing what moves us, what inspires us, what uplifts us or depresses us, what happened to us in the past that we try to compensate for in the present, and what we wish for our future, is the formula for self-awareness.

To be effective in the struggle to know ourselves, we must identify our inner psychological workings. We must overcome our defenses and avoid excuses as we behold our true selves. *We need to see ourselves in the third person.*

This kind of insight can spring only from our inborn voice of conscience. Be sincere with yourself, tune out the false external voices, and get to the heart of matters through self-talk by saying,

I have always been perplexed at the disparity between who I want to be and the person I end up becoming. Why is it that I plan to do one thing but invariably do something completely different? Where is my discipline? Where is my self-control? What demon seizes me and prevents me from mastering my actions?

I want to create my own destiny, but I always end up a prisoner of fate. Forces beyond my control seem to possess me and steer me away from my intended destination.

Yet there's no such thing as ghosts. I have not been seized by a dybbuk, nor am I possessed by a malign spirit. I know that the forces do not lie outside of me but inside.

I am constantly blaming external causes for my predicament. I disempower myself by imagining that things outside of me have dominion over me. I have made myself servile and subordinate.

The time has come to admit that forces and inclinations exist inside me that I have yet to identify. They seem to work through me and control my actions—but no longer. To name them and learn how to master them, I have to become far more introspective and self-aware. It's time for me to conquer my defenses and get to know myself.

Self-mastery is the product of self-knowledge, and I am ready now to take the first steps toward achieving it.

Unlike an ordinary, unthinking animal, all human beings possess the unique capacity to hold their own lives in the palms of their hands, examining themselves as if they were strangers. In so doing, we can examine ourselves for defects, correct them, and begin to heal.

The people who are capable of doing this, of overcoming the defense mechanisms that would make them turn away or shift blame elsewhere, gain true mastery over their lives. They alone are capable of becoming the individuals they set out to be. They are what the *Zohar* calls *Aspaklaria Hameirah*—a translucent window. They have the gift of seeing to the core of themselves and evaluating their true essence.

Why "translucent," you may wonder—why not go all the way and become fully transparent? After all, we live in the age of Facebook, where concerns about privacy seem to have become obsolete. The answer is that baring your every thought and deed is just another form of narcissism. Not only that, it's dangerous: by opening yourself up to the world, you cheapen yourself, rendering your entire life ordinary.

Far better to become translucent, holding your own life in the palm of your hand, while keeping your secrets respectably close to your chest.

How do you achieve translucence in your life? How do you see yourself in the third person in practice?

First, you must be prepared to be vulnerable to yourself. You have to be bold enough to embark on an investigation that will probably uncover things that will literally repel you. When you criticize yourself, your natural survival instinct will immediately kick in. Your personality will respond as if to a physical assault. To overcome these innate reactions requires courage. It is no small matter to push past your personality's gag reflex. Yet in this lies another phenomenal human ability that animals lack: namely, the capacity to switch off our natural defense mechanisms and become self-critical.

Find your voice of conscience deep inside the everyday cacophony. Once you've located it, ask yourself,

What do I feel when I receive criticism? Much as I'd like to think that I take it in stride, the truth is that even the mildest critique is perceived to be an attack. When my boss tells me that my work isn't up to snuff, my hackles rise. If somebody looks at me the wrong way on the street, I feel upset and wonder what's wrong with me. Is it my clothes? My hair? What have I done wrong? Loving criticism from my family members feels like a psychological assault. And even now that I'm investigating it within myself, I feel my hackles rising, as though my own self-talk were a kind of attack!

Yet to defy your natural defenses, to be able to *invite* such an attack, even initiate it yourself as you seek out and correct the corrosion within your character, is an uncanny and remarkable human ability. To find this kind of talent, you must confront your deepest insecurities—a difficult road but, in the end, a rewarding one.

After mustering up the initial courage to push past your natural survival instinct, you need to seek a better vantage point. How else can you behold yourself as if from afar? To rise above yourself, you have to learn to distinguish between the higher and lower aspects of your personality. One side of you is the everyday part that lives life unthinkingly. The other side is the higher part, which is capable of cognition, understanding, and, yes, even transcendence.

One of the most famous stories in the Bible is about the Jews who built a golden calf. They took gold with them as they left Egypt and with it forged a statue of a calf. To make them atone for their brazen idolatry, God commanded that they build a golden tabernacle. Yet the question arose: where would this gold come from? All of the gold had gone into creating the calf, so how could they construct an entirely new tabernacle from nothing?

The ancient rabbis explained that everybody has a tiny measure of gold socked away somewhere for a rainy day, whether it's a nugget of gold hidden in his pocket or a savings account with a few extra bucks. The Jews contributed their emergency gold to build the tabernacle, thus fulfilling God's wishes.

This gold is more than a precious metal; it's a metaphor that represents the precious substance that is hidden deep inside us. We begin life filled to the brim with gold. As we age and get more materialistic, pettier, more jealous, and distracted by life, we spend that gold. Yet no matter how far gone we may seem, there is still a tiny nugget of gold hidden away within. It is our innocence, our goodness. Whenever we seek to change our lives, as did the Jews forging a golden tabernacle from their emergency stores of gold, we draw from this source.

When I talk about seeing yourself in the third person, that's what I mean. You must recede into the small part of yourself that is most precious and incorruptible. Untainted by worldly experience, it provides you with your share of transcendence.

So, let's say you manage to push through your defenses and view yourself from afar. The picture of yourself in the third person is coming into view, yet you still have no sense of scale. That's because the third item you need is a yardstick, a barometer by which to judge yourself. This is the precise role of the voice of conscience: it represents both the whisper of what you ought to be and the map that will always guide you faithfully back to your source.

Finally, here's the most important part. *No excuses*. Even after you've achieved the transcendence you sought, it's nearly impossible to overcome your natural defenses, designed as they are to protect your personality from assault. At the last second, a shrill voice will shout accusingly, "But wait, you're not really a negative person—everyone around you is actually at fault!" Or, "Now hold on; you're not being overly critical of your kids. You're the parent, and it's their job to hear and obey!"

How can you fix an issue when you always blame it on someone else? What you're experiencing is the last vestige of the gag reflex. Whereas at first, it told you to stop looking at yourself, at the last moment it tries to triumphantly declare the matter someone else's fault. You didn't do anything, so why should you have to change? It was done to you, so you must be the victim.

Once, while I was writing my weekly column, my wife asked me if I knew where a lost receipt was. I immediately became upset. I told her that I was writing on a deadline, and it was wrong for her to bother me with something so petty. Didn't she understand I was trying to concentrate? She apologized and left the room.

Within five minutes, I was overcome by two sharp feelings. The first was embarrassment and remorse that I had gotten upset at my own wife over an innocent question. I had to go and apologize immediately. The second was a feeling of confusion. What had just happened?

I attempted to look within myself for answers, mustering up courage, transcending myself, and calling on my voice of conscience as a guide. Even so, part of me continued to assert that I had lashed out because of simple annoyance at being disrupted from my work. As easy as it would have been to believe this, I had to continually remind myself that the final step of seeing yourself in the third person is *no excuses*.

I interrogated myself, and soon enough I realized what had happened. In that instant I had been filled with arrogance. Here I was, a writer, being bothered by life's trifling details. Was it right to pull me down from the mountaintop to talk about the tiny vagaries of life? Me, this great thinker. And why was I so arrogant at that moment? Because I have always wrestled with issues of self-esteem. I need my writing and my columns to validate my existence. I need this book you're reading right now to feel that I matter. At that moment, I thought my wife was taking it away from me.

I lashed out because I felt that she was turning me into an *ordinary* husband who stacks receipts somewhere. I thought that I was above such trivialities.

I began to converse with my inner voice of conscience, and what I said was very simple: "*The truth is, my greatest fear is that I am ordinary.* When I lash out at someone as loving as my wife, it's just because I am running from the terrifying confirmation of that fact: that we're all special, and yet we're also ordinary. Those who fear they are pygmies run from small things to giant things because they are intimidated by their own inner smallness—and that's just what's happened to me."

The strangest thing is that the essence of a defense mechanism is to protect you, yet it is fundamentally disempowering to blame everything on others. To find the truth, you must push through such defenses, guiding yourself through self-talk. Only then can you reap the benefits of becoming translucent: you will become capable of true healing at last.

Whenever you behave in a way that is obscure to you, whenever you feel yourself losing control, try to see yourself in the third person. Overcome your natural resistance, transcend the lower parts of yourself, cue up your voice of conscience, find the resolve to defy your gag reflex, and ask yourself:

What motivates me? Why do I work so hard? Who exactly am I trying to impress?

Every day I find myself climbing some new mountain. Although it may leave me with a glimmer of self-satisfaction, I find that my life with my family still suffers. No wonder: I have expended my principal energies at work. By the time I return home, I'm running on fumes.

But now I'm starting to see the truth. When I look at myself in the third person, from afar, I see someone who is always trying to prove himself. I begin every day with a deficiency mentality: my cup is half empty, rather than half full. I've lived my entire life with a spirit of inadequacy, never feeling that I belong or that I am smart enough, attractive enough, charismatic enough, or interesting enough to command the affection of my peers. And I have compensated by making myself into a slave.

College acceptance boards, teachers, professors, bosses, VIPs at cocktail parties—I'll do whatever it takes to please them. It seems as if the only people I ignore are those who mean the most to me. I have sought to be a success in everyone's eyes except my family's. But let's be honest, why do I care about impressing anyone *except* my family? If in life I end up being a hero to the whole world but a failure in the eyes of my spouse and children, has my life really been successful?

Am I really a success if the people who mean
the most to me think the least of me?

When you fail to see yourself in the third person, the window that should be translucent becomes obscured and smudged. As a result, your life can end up going seriously off track.

Look at the politicians who run for office in this country. If you ask politicians point-blank why they are running, they'll tell you that they want to serve their country, their state, their community. Fair enough, but that's not the whole truth, of course. Most politicians run for office because they want power. They want to feel important. Being an elected official gives them meaning and purpose.

Serving the public good allows you to contribute and make a difference in countless people's lives. It should stand to reason that if you're a senator and you run for president and lose, you still have an opportunity to contribute. Yet when you become single-mindedly obsessed with the office, you lose track of what you were working for in the first place. Then if you lose an election, you think your life has come to an end.

The same thing can happen to your marriage. An image can easily overwhelm your reality if you're not careful. Maurice had been married to Bettina for twelve years when Bettina walked in on Maurice in the marital bed and saw him masturbating to porn on his laptop. Afterward, he confessed that he masturbates three to five times a day. Bettina was deeply insulted and felt that this was why her husband rarely touched her. She asked me to counsel her husband.

He said to me, "I'm going to tell you something that I can never tell my wife. I have never liked her body. When we married, she had tiny breasts, and I wasn't attracted to them. To make me happy, she had a breast enlargement. But I hate fake breasts even more. Her whole petite body type has no appeal to me. So I look at pornographic images of voluptuous, large-breasted women. It's pathetic to have to masturbate at night, but I feel constrained in this marriage. I want to be free. I'm an attractive man."

He was blaming his wife for his lack of attraction. In his mind, it was not his fault but hers. Yet the boredom came entirely from Maurice. Rather than work on creating greater erotic lust in his marriage—by using, for example, the mental tools I discuss in my book *The Kosher Sutra*: *Eight Sacred Secrets for Reigniting Desire and Restoring Passion for Life*—he instead became dependent on fantasy images outside of his marriage. Men like Maurice often end up miserable and alone. It was far easier for Maurice to look at pictures of naked women than to look deeply into himself to gain greater self-knowledge.

The medieval Jewish sage Maimonides said that there are three stages to repentance. The first is acknowledgment of error. The second is confession of sin. And the third is changing one's way and rejoining a righteous path. Step number one is that which begins the whole process. So, if Maurice's problems resemble yours in any way, resolve to see yourself in the third person, and muster up the courage to acknowledge and admit to error in self-talk. Say to yourself,

I have made the mistake of neglecting my family. My kids often have to repeat themselves three times before I hear them. Even with a beautiful family, I sometimes see myself as a failure because I am using material possessions to define my success. It's time for me to stop lusting after all that I don't have. I have an impressive gift to contribute to the world and to my family, and I'm going to refocus on giving myself to those who matter most to me. I resolve to become translucent and to weed out the defense mechanisms that prevent me from seeing what I'm really doing. From now on, I'm going to pay attention to my family and, in particular, give my spouse all of the affection she/he deserves.

Don't get me wrong: self-awareness isn't easy. In fact, for most of us it's a huge hill to climb. To surpass their defense mechanisms and see themselves in the third person, most people must come to grips with serious cognitive dissonance. Even the most brilliant among us can fail to overcome his own resistance; a great example of this is Albert Einstein.

Long after enunciating the principle of relativity, Einstein found himself stuck in a scientific rut. His colleagues were making great advancements in physics, while he was treading water. The reason: he refused to believe that the principles of quantum mechanics could be true. He couldn't accept the unpredictability of subatomic particles, because he firmly believed in an ordered universe. The implications of chaos were just too painful for him to admit. As a result, he couldn't see the truth and found himself being left behind by the science he loved. In this case, insight failed even the greatest genius of the twentieth century.

It's incredibly difficult at times to become truly translucent. Yet to make a real change and see yourself with new, objective eyes, it's necessary to make the effort—especially for parents, who so easily pass along their own personal problems, faulty motivations, and negative inner voices to their children.

A woman named Janice came to me seeking help in determining the source of her children's anger. She had two daughters, ages eighteen and seventeen, who fought constantly. As I spent time in Janice's home trying to get a read on the situation, I discovered that their anger came from, you guessed it, Janice herself. To be sure, Janice's rage was more subdued than her daughters'. She did not scream; more often she simmered. She gave ferociously hostile looks and shut her daughters down that way.

I sat with Janice and said, "Let me explain why your children are so easily offended. Imagine that you have a broken toe. You stubbed it against the kitchen table, and it's all black and blue. Along comes a baby's foot, as light as a feather. When it treads on your toe, you're going to scream. The toe is already so bruised and broken that anything that happens to it will hurt.

"The same applies to your kids. There's an undercurrent of anger running through the entire household. So anything they do to each other, even the slightest misstep on the other's toes, is a provocation. Everyone in your home is wounded. *And the source is you.* So you need to discuss with me your own anger and how we can help you recognize it in yourself."

Yet Janice denied that she was angry. She refused to believe that something was boiling over inside her. Forget the fact that her father had abandoned her when she was seven years old. Disregard the detail that her husband cheated on her repeatedly until she left him. Janice had a painful life, but the pain made her blind. It was easiest for her simply to ignore it.

Just as Einstein couldn't admit the chaos of the universe, Janice could not acknowledge the disarray in her own heart.

Her problem was that she was unaware. She had not been trained to overcome her innate resistance to seeing herself in the third person. Becoming translucent to yourself, however, is *never* only about you—it always has ramifications on the people around you, on your spouse, your children. Only by finding your way to self-awareness can you raise children who are free of your own defense mechanisms and emotional complications.

Tell yourself wholeheartedly, in your inner voice of conscience, the truth about how you relate to your kids:

Sometimes I find myself being very hard on my children. Rather than complimenting them and showing them affection, I seem only to look for faults. I've tried to figure out why. I've talked myself into thinking that I do it because I love them and want what's best for them, but I will no longer be satisfied with weak explanations like these.

No, I realize that something else is at work. If I were really doing this for their benefit, I would offer praise rather than criticism. It would be even easier to excuse my behavior by saying that I'm doing it because my father did it to me, and his father did it to him, all the way back for countless generations. But that's a cop-out as well, and I am going to do all that I can to cease blaming other people for my shortcomings.

The real reason I criticize my children is because it bothers me that they have it easier than I did. They don't have to struggle as much as I did, because I made the sacrifices for them. I worked hard so that my kids would have a better life. Now I am, in a strange way, inflicting my pain on my children. I take it out on them, when in truth they did nothing to deserve this. I'm just passing along my bitterness.

It sounds odd that a parent could be jealous of his/her own children. And it pains me to have to admit it. It's humiliating. But only by having the courage to probe deeply into my motivation can I become the master of my actions.

From now on, I will choose not to criticize—and when I do, I will maintain a ratio where compliments far exceed criticisms in number. From now on when I slip up and yell at my children, I'll apologize. I'll be open with them and admit my own failings, so that they will be able to achieve self-awareness sooner than I was able to. Most of all, even when I have negative feelings toward my children, I will see it happening to myself, as if from the third person. In so doing, I will take the first and most difficult step toward changing these emotions and feeling nothing but unbridled joy for my children.

. . .

Our earliest inklings of self-awareness and consciousness can arrive in flashes of clarity and inspiration. I will never forget the first time I achieved translucence and saw myself in the third person. When I was seven years old, my family wasn't exactly poor, but we were pretty close. Despite my parents' efforts, I knew that most of my peers in school had so much more than I did. That knowledge made me self-conscious and a bit embarrassed.

One day, the teacher walked into the classroom and gave us each a book catalog. We were going to order books for outside reading. "Go home to your parents and see which books they'll let you buy." My mother told me we could afford to buy only a single book. But I knew that I would feel ashamed the next day, so I did something that I knew was manipulative.

I went to my father and asked him for money to buy six books. He said, "If you really want them, we'll get them." Even at that age, I knew perfectly well what I was up to. I was playing my parents against each other. My father, who felt that we kids were closer to my mother, was showing that he accommodated me when my mother didn't. My mother complained that I did not need the books, nor would I even read them. But I had a big smile on my face the next day when my classmates couldn't believe I was ordering the most books in the class. When the books arrived, the other kids looked on in envy. I was rich at last. On my bookcase, the books quickly gathered dust. After a few days, it was as if nothing had changed.

Except for me. I knew what I had done. I knew I was not innocent. And I vowed never to be the cause of friction between my parents again. It was my first moment of true self-awareness, and I still think of it, even today.

Nevertheless, I continued to nurse a feeling of inadequacy during my childhood and young adulthood. I repeatedly tried to prove myself, not always in the most healthful ways. I have come a long way since those days, but such feelings have never completely left me. I don't know that I will ever be completely cured, even as I have made enormous progress. But the self-awareness that began when I was seven years old has nevertheless helped save me.

Yet it's so darn lonely and scary to go into that dark place of self-awareness. It pulls us away from the pack and into ourselves. We feel isolated and alone, and who knows what we might find there? What if we find something we hate? Or something we cannot confront? One is reminded of the famous Jack Nicholson line from *A Few Good Men*: "You can't handle the truth." Who among us is seriously prepared to confront the dark and terrible truth of our own imperfections and inadequacy?

Even so, self-awareness is not an option but a necessity. Without gaining access to that dark and difficult place inside ourselves, without self-criticizing and transcending our lower selves, we'll never become the people we want to be. So look at yourself from afar and behold your feelings of insignificance, your sorrows, and your regrets. Then interrogate them in self-talk. If you're willing to dig deeply enough, you can solve any problem.

If you feel out of shape, ugly, or unattractive, say to yourself,

I have always wondered why I feel so ugly. I look in the mirror and see a body that is too fat, too flabby, too old. Hair that is too gray. A face that is too lined. Skin that is too loose. No matter what outfit I wear, I always think I look bad. When I look at other people, I'm jealous of their youth, their strength, some little quality about them that I don't have.

But by looking at myself in the third person, I am coming to understand that objectively, I cannot look terrible in everything I put on. My revulsion at my reflection in the mirror is nothing more than irrational self-loathing.

Why do I feel so bad about myself? It's because I punish myself on the outside for things I feel on the inside. I have bought into society's lie that the only measures of beauty are smooth skin and muscle tone. My daily intake is not healthy. My values come from a steady diet of magazines, TV, and movies, and I have become a more superficial person as a result. I do not value my heart or my mind enough. I fear that the people I meet couldn't care less about my inner qualities and judge me immediately for my looks, my money, my social standing. That's why I know it's time for me to find a healthier environment, one that goes deeper and values human beings in their entirety.

Yet that's just the beginning. If you continue to peel away the layers, you'll surely find that your distress boils down to a general unhappiness with the world. Search out the roots of your unhappiness by asking yourself,

Why am I always so irrationally unhappy? I have so many blessings, but I don't seem to value them. Instead, I'm always waiting for some big thing to happen to me that will make me happy. My next relationship will finally bring me happiness. My next promotion will make me feel like a success. Maybe I'll even win the lottery while I'm at it.

It's almost as if something has to happen outside of me to bring me joy. I now realize that I have utterly disempowered myself by making my happiness dependent on things that I cannot control. The Declaration of Independence says I have a right to the pursuit of happiness, and it's a right I believe in deeply. But if it can only come from things outside my control, then I have no such right. Then I am at the mercy of others for this most fundamental of human rights.

I now recognize that my lack of happiness is the result of an unnatural dependency on people, events, and things. Happiness comes from finding meaning and purpose. Only men and women who feel as if they belong, who have found their place in the universe and are making a meaningful contribution, are happy and content. Those who have not found this need the endless distractions of objects they own and people they conquer to bring them fleeting happiness.

I resolve to change my life's goal. No longer will I devote myself to a career—from now on, my focus will be on finding a calling. An obsession with my career is killing me because it makes me dependent on an arbitrary scale of success to indicate whether I am valuable. But a calling, in which my life has meaning based on the contribution I make to those in need, is a real and intrinsic barometer of success. There is nothing arbitrary about it.

I don't want to live for others' opinions about me. I want to live for my principles, for God, and for those who matter most to me. So, yes, I want to succeed professionally, but I want to do it because I have gifts, potential, and something to contribute. Not because I crave acceptance. If I do it for that reason, then I have made others—complete strangers—my masters, and I risk squandering all that is valuable to me. What's the point of being a hero to the world if I end up a stranger to my own wife and kids?

Your marriage is the most important relationship in your life. Inertia can easily set in—but your marriage can also be dramatically improved and re-enlivened if you can manage to see yourself in the third person. Make a promise to yourself, in conversation with your inner voice:

I am making a commitment to get to know myself much better. There can be no empowerment without self-knowledge. I want to know what motivates me, what pushes me, what makes me do what I do. This is the only way that I can get complete control of my life. I can't be someone who is governed by others.

I know that my marriage often operates on cruise control, that my spouse and I watch much more TV than we talk, that we make love for only a few minutes a week, and that the majority of our conversations are practical, rather than intimate. We love each other, but it's become more of an assumption than something consciously experienced. We know there's love down there if you dig, but on the surface it's barely perceptible.

I used to think this was just the inevitable decline that all couples experience. Time goes on, you get into a routine, and everything becomes just a little bit stale. But now such simple assumptions are beneath me. Thinking about it more deeply, I understand that I have been blaming my spouse, however subtly, for the fact that so many of my dreams never materialized.

I always thought it would be different, that I would be one of those people with a truly glamorous life. I imagined my house being bigger, my car fancier. I envisioned taking exotic vacations a few times a year around the world. I figured I would have perfect kids who listened to me, like on the *Brady Bunch*. I saw myself with fewer gray hairs and fewer pounds. But here I am, and it all seems kind of ordinary. We struggle to pay our mortgage. When we do fly, we fly coach. Our kids are great, but it's a daily struggle to raise them. And I'm getting older. The only glamour I seem to have in my life is talking about celebrities and reading *People* magazine.

I subconsciously blame my spouse for the failure of glamorous things to materialize. In other words, I've come to realize that I harbor hostility to my spouse, as if he/she is the reason that my dreams weren't fulfilled.

I now understand just how immature I've been acting. My lofty dreams were based on erroneous and superficial values. They were substitutions for the love and commitment I was looking for all along. Now, look at what my life has amounted to: I have a spouse who has built a life with me and children who, though not perfect, are beautiful and miraculous. I don't know what I would do without them.

My family's love sustains me. I have bought into the lie that relationships and love don't matter as much as a private jet and a weekend mansion. To find my way to new values, I need a new pair of eyes. I need courage, transcendence, a voice of conscience, and "no excuses" will be my byword on the road to translucence.

I need to see myself in the third person, and it's already happening, already within my grasp. I don't want to be one of those people who values his/her blessings only when he/she is in danger, God forbid, of losing them.

To develop a personalized relationship with your inner voice of conscience, ask yourself the following questions. Respond to them, and let the answers guide you on self-talks of your own devising.

Am I objective about my faults? Do I get defensive when, in the course of everyday life, my flaws emerge? Or do I accept criticism or even go so far as to self-criticize?

Do I point out everyone else's problems but my own? Do I listen to the inner voices that justify my actions, or do I heed the voice of conscience that reveals the truth?

Am I capable of identifying things about myself that need to change? Do I recognize the need to transcend myself and hold my life in the palm of my hand?

Am I truly fulfilling my potential, conquering obstacles externally and internally, and becoming all that I can be?

7

Be a Blessing, Not a Burden

CONVERSATION 7

There is enough darkness in the world already;
I should be a source of light.

For the last 250 or so years, Americans have tried just about every-thing to find happiness. After all, it's our birthright, isn't it? As Jefferson put it in our Declaration of Independence, "Life, liberty, and the pursuit of happiness." Yet it's one thing to tell people they have the right to be happy and quite another to reveal *how* they can achieve it.

So we have sought shortcuts. First on our list is the acquisition of money and property. As a result, America has become the richest country in the world. Yet that wealth has come at a cost, for, accord-ing to the *Washington Post*, Americans consume three-quarters of the world's antidepressants. Clearly, the money thing hasn't worked out all that well.

Some have thought to find happiness in sexual conquests, power, and fame. Still others have applied themselves to more spiritual pursuits such as religion, meditation, and yoga. No doubt, the latter quests are more fulfilling than fruitless hunts for sex and celebrity, but even they do not provide the real secret of happiness.

Thomas Jefferson was a genius, a visionary, and a patriot, but his understanding of the search for happiness was dead wrong. Happiness is not something that can be stumbled upon, like a lost wallet. Nor is it a destination toward which you can march, hoping one day you will arrive. You simply can't *pursue* happiness—the more you try, the more it escapes you. It's kind of like attempting to fall asleep. The harder you try, the more elusive it becomes.

Here, then, is the secret of happiness.

Happiness is the by-product, the automatic outcome,
and the organic result of a purposeful life.

When you have a purpose, you achieve happiness. And when you feel unnecessary, directionless—when your life is filled with mean-inglessness, when you question your impact or feel irrelevant—you cannot be happy. That's when you turn to silly and unimportant dis-tractions to fill the void.

Take shopping, for example. Studies show that the number one cure for depression in America—the thing that most often makes us consistently happy—is impulse buying. But how happy does it make you? Isn't it true that you feel happy for a few hours and then instantly start feeling depressed again? That's what makes shopping an addiction. You have to consistently up the hit.

Think about the times that you have been most happy. Consult your inner voice of conscience and ask yourself,

Have promotions, bonuses, and successful investments made me happy? How about blowing my paycheck on expensive new gadgets and tropical vacations or gorging myself on junk food or trash TV? Well, they've been pleasant—or so it seemed at the time. But as soon as they were over, little happiness remained. In fact, these distractions seemed to create a dependency. I needed more and more of them as time went on.

The truth is, I feel most content when I have a purpose. When I'm helping my kids with their homework, I feel good about myself. I feel purposeful. When I put my arm around my wife and make her feel loved and see her smile, I feel content. When I stop in the street to give a homeless person a dollar and tell him, "God bless you," I feel at peace with my conscience. Being a good, useful person is true happiness for me.

Absolutely right! This is the true secret: happiness is the organic outcome of a life that is a blessing to others.

That's why you must live your life as a blessing, not as a burden.

I'm sure you've met people who are burdens on others. America has more than a few of them. Bitterness about life's unfairness causes them to envy those who are happier. They gossip about other people and sow discord among their friends. They may recognize that they are unhappy, but they haven't a clue how to improve their life's lot. Moreover, they are blissfully unaware that their dysfunction is contagious.

Rebecca is a grown woman who takes offense every time her parents give gifts to her sister, Amy. She always compares her own gifts to what Amy has received. Rebecca's griping and jealousy were tearing the family apart. Her parents asked her to come speak to me, in the hope that I could help her.

I said to her, "I understand why you're doing this. It's not about money. It's about love. You feel as though you haven't received an adequate amount of love from your parents. As a result, whenever your parents give gifts to someone else, to you it means they love that person more.

"But, Rebecca, look—it's bad enough that you can't accept your sister's getting a gift. More serious is the fact that you're inflicting your fears on everyone around you. Unless you make a conscious effort to change, you will make the mistake of a living life as a burden on others, rather than as a blessing."

People like Rebecca aren't inherently bad, but they are unquestionably broken. If they were to identify the root cause of their unhappiness and make themselves aware of why they are unhappy, they could gradually remove the suffering from their lives. In so doing, they would cease being a burden to others as well.

I'm not saying that you're a broken person. I have no doubt that you do your best, trying not to let your unhappiness spill onto others. But we all face the same choices, the same opportunities, and the same hurdles, regardless of whether we're saints. Being a blessing to others requires constant commitment and attention, even for the best among us.

Engage your true voice of conscience, and let it guide you in self-talk. Say,

> I recognize that my pursuit of happiness has left me exhausted. I work so hard for my family, yet sometimes I feel as though my attempts to be a good person fall flat.
>
> I am always asking myself, "Should I break out of my routine and do something simple and good for my fellow man?" Maybe today a homeless person is asking for a buck, or one of my coworkers needs a ride home. Yet even though I know the answer should be yes, it's hard to beat the inertia of my life, so I fail to be a blessing, time and again.
>
> But no matter how busy I am or what my mood is like, these daily trials shouldn't stop me. I know that the real questions are: Which path will I pursue? Will I be a source of strife or a source of peace? And will I increase people's happiness or serve as a source of pain in their lives?
>
> *Will I be a burden or a blessing?*

Ask yourself that crucial question if you want to know the source of true happiness. Answering the question correctly is the essence of this chapter.

. . .

Let's talk about that choice—and all of the ways it presents itself to us.

Remember when you were a child, attending grade school. Every once in a while, a substitute teacher took over for the day. Think back: how did you react? Did you make trouble for the teacher just for the sake of getting a laugh?

I remember being in class and knowing that I had that choice. I could be one of the respectful kids who knew that the teacher needed all of the help she could get. Yet after my parents' divorce, I wanted more than anything to be liked. The best shortcut I could think of was to be the class clown who made other kids laugh. Today I regret it. You know why? Because I now have nine children in school, and I want them to get an education. And I hope there isn't a kid in their class who is messing it up for them the way I sometimes did for my classmates.

Facing up to the challenge of being a blessing is rarely easy. But if you consult your inner voice of conscience, you'll have little choice but to do the right thing.

Let's say your family is getting together for the holidays, and you're going to have to sit down with your brother-in-law, whom you've been avoiding for years. It's not an uncommon situation. Studies show that two of the times when families fight most are, paradoxically, Thanksgiving and Christmas. All of the grudges and hurt that people have carried for years come to the fore.

You can't stand this guy. Your hatred has been boiling up inside you ever since your sister married him years ago. As you're driving over to the holiday dinner, you hear a voice, instantly recognizable as the voice of your negative emotions, testing the waters: "How gratifying would it be to make nasty little comments that show everyone that I hold them in contempt? If I do, it's sure to create a poisonous atmosphere for all who are gathered. But what do I care? I hate the man. He never apologized for his past behavior. I'm not a doormat, after all. Why should I let him treat me any way he wants without fighting back?"

Dinner hasn't even started, and you've already reached a fork in the road. You can be a burden, allowing the bile to spill over onto the entire family, or you can be a blessing, transcending the slight and remembering all of the nice things your brother-in-law has done for your sister.

To make that choice, you need to drown out the voices of jealousy, revenge, and anger and find your way back to your innermost voice of conscience. Converse with it and say,

> Do I want to be a burden or a blessing? I have the ability to heal myself of the poison coursing through my veins. But just as easily, like a serpent, I could bite others and spread the poison around.
>
> Do I want to score petty points on this guy and make everyone at dinner uncomfortable? Or do I want to have an incredible evening with the people I love?

When you frame it that way, how could you do otherwise than be a blessing?

Imagine that your two best friends have recently had a tiff. You talk to one of them, and he reels off a list of all of the reasons the other guy is a scoundrel. Let your inner voice of conscience frame the choice that confronts you and say to yourself,

> My two dearest friends are already burdened by the brokenness of their relationship. Am I going to increase the burden by bad-mouthing the other guy? Or do I have the grace to smooth over their conflict and try to make things better between them?

Say you've had a long, hard day at work. You come home spent. What's worse, you walk in and dinner isn't ready, the house is a mess, and nobody says hello. Ta-da: the ATM has arrived and no one even seems to care. How could they ignore you like this? Don't they know how you've been slaving all day for them? How are you going to behave?

Find the voice of conscience inside yourself and ask yourself,

Am I the kind of person who creates turmoil in my own home? Am I really going to unleash on my family the hardships of my day? I can already see the future. If I make a habit of burdening them this way, fast-forward a few years and my kids won't even want to speak to me. They'll avoid me at all costs, because I suck the oxygen out of the house every time I walk in the door.

No. *I refuse to indulge in being a burden.* As hard as it is to overcome my natural feelings of fatigue and grouchiness, I will make the effort to brighten up the home with my presence.

A blessing is someone who brings light to a dark space. A burden is someone who only brings more darkness. He doesn't try to help people unload their problems. He is a narcissist who puts himself at the center of his own moral universe. If he is in pain, he spreads it around to everyone else. If he isn't having fun, then why should you? And if he feels that no one loves him, then he's going to make darn sure that you don't feel loved either.

Sandra came to me for counseling. Her husband, Greg, became infatuated with virtually every young woman who worked for him in his law office. Sandra found the e-mails he was sending them. As she told me about them, she actually giggled. Nervous laughter, to be sure, but still, she giggled. When her husband arrived, I told him, "In all of the years I've done marital counseling, I have never heard a woman giggle while she read e-mails to me that her husband has sent to other women telling them he loved them. The reason is that you have so humiliated her with your behavior that she can deal with it only by pretending it's something flippant and humorous. Were she to confront the full reality of her pain, she might never recover."

As I said this, Sandra was no longer giggling but crying. Her mascara was running down her face. I said to her husband, "A man is supposed to make his wife feel sensual and beautiful. But your wife barely even objects to your serial infatuations with other women. You have made her feel so ugly and so inadequate that she doesn't even feel she has the right to object. She can't compete, so what right does she have to stop you? That's the extent to which you have become not a blessing but a burden to your wife.

"But you can change. You can recognize that all of the attention you have lavished on other women comes from your own inner brokenness, rather than being a result of some flaw in your wife. You can apologize to her, give her unconditional affection, and make her feel whole again."

Let your internal voices be your secret weapon in fending off burdensome behavior. During self-talk, repeat the following commitments:

> I want to connect with people. I don't want to be detached.
>
> I want to listen and not always have to be right. I don't have to be the one to have the final word in an argument.
>
> I want to be empathetic, able to feel someone else's position, rather than judging him or her.
>
> I want to have an open mind, open to others and to their ideas.
>
> I want to be gracious. I want to bestow dignity on others and make them feel important.
>
> I want to reward, not punish, the people who are good to me—no matter whether they're my parents, my spouse, my boss, my coworkers, or my children.
>
> I want to inspire others and, through that, be inspired.

If you can commit to these simple aspirations, you'll be well on your way to becoming a blessing, rather than a burden.

We all know what being a burden looks like. We see it every day. The alternative, however, is far more rare. What does it mean to be a blessing in the real world?

Not long ago, I was working at a TV network when financial hardship set in. The managers laid off a lot of people at once and treated a woman named Elizabeth very shabbily. After the sad news broke, Elizabeth's colleagues came over to commiserate about how awfully the management had behaved. Everyone was eager to hear her trash her former bosses, but she didn't take the bait. This amazing woman instead chose to be a blessing.

Elizabeth told everyone that there was no sense in being bitter. Absolutely, it was sad that she would have leave, but there was a recession on, and we had to be realistic about cutting costs. Some people were going to lose their jobs. We had all learned so much from one another and had such a great time. Now we had to be understanding of the tough choices the company had to make to survive. Even after losing her job, Elizabeth stepped up and acted like a blessing to her work environment. She left behind a legacy of high moral stature and peace.

Fundamentally, the key to being a blessing is choosing righteousness. You don't have to be Mother Teresa or Nelson Mandela, martyring yourself for some great cause. You just have to do the right thing. It can be as simple as holding the door for a stranger or giving your spouse an unprompted compliment.

It's not hard to figure out what to do. The difficult thing is overcoming your impatience, your stress and anxiety, and being a blessing even when you don't feel like it. As hard as it sometimes is, in being a blessing you will find a level of freedom you never thought possible; nothing will uplift you more than the feeling that you are a positive force in others' lives.

Be honest with yourself. Engage your inner voice of conscience in self-talk and say,

I know for a fact that I am a decent person. I do all of the big stuff right.

Family is important to me. I work hard to support my spouse and children. Now that my parents are getting older, I try to be there for them, even though I feel pressed between two generations who need care. I'm also a decent friend. When people I care about are in need, I try to be there for them. I listen to them when they're down and try to lift them up.

I also do my best to cultivate a religious and spiritual life, although probably not as much as I should. I go to church, volunteer for causes that are important when I have the time, and in general try to act selflessly.

I illuminate darkness wherever I find it, I smile and make my coworkers happier, I work hard and contribute at work, and I go out of my way to show respect to the people who help in my home. When someone is in trouble or in pain, it hurts me, and I try to do something about it, however small.

In all of those things I'm a blessing. I make my kids feel special, and I make my spouse feel loved. Had I never been born, all of these people whose lives I touch would not have my blessings in their lives.

Yet on the other hand, I can't deny that I sometimes, maybe even a lot of the time, can be a burden to people. Sometimes when my mother calls me, I'm impatient on the phone. I have a lot to do. The kids are screaming, dinner's in the oven, and I show my irritation. After the fact, I feel regret. My mother deserved better. I have made her feel as if she's not important to me. How could I be so rude to the woman who sacrificed so much for me?

That's not all. At times I lose my temper and yell at my kids. They ask me questions over and over again, and rather than be impressed at their curiosity, I'll splutter, "Not now," and see the smiles instantly disappear from their faces. I'm sometimes even a burden to my spouse. I come home in a bad mood, and I take it out on him/her. Dinner won't be ready, and I'll grumble. I know it's not fair, but I can't help giving in to being a burden sometimes.

As much as I love my friends, I also love to gossip. Sometimes we'll all be sitting around talking and I'll repeat a disparaging story about an acquaintance that puts the person in a negative light.

Once we depart, I know I've been a burden to someone who didn't deserve it. The person wasn't there to defend himself/herself, and I surely don't even know the whole story. I gossiped only because it made me feel good about myself to put other people down. And that right there is the quintessential form of being a burden. Why should I saddle some innocent person with my issues?

Finally, I know I'm not as grateful as I should be. So many people have been good to me and have helped me get to where I am, from teachers who went beyond the call of duty to inspire me to bosses who promoted me when others objected to people who lent me money or time when they didn't have to. But once I got what I wanted, I failed to be gracious. I didn't stay in touch. How hard would it have been to simply send a Christmas card or give them a once-a-year phone call to show that I remember their kindness?

To all of these people I could have been a blessing, but I was not. And by not being a blessing, again I have to admit, I became a burden. I know how I feel when people are burdens on me—the darkness chokes off my goodness, and I swear never to help anyone else again.

I no longer have any illusions about life and what my purpose on earth is. First and foremost, it's to be a source of light in the darkness. That's why I want to recommit to being a blessing.

Doing the right thing isn't the hardest part of being a blessing. The main difficulty is overcoming the urge *not* to be a blessing. Avoiding complacency is the real challenge.

Just today I was walking down the street. Already, I was late for a TV interview. Literally, two different cell phones were ringing, and I was on the way to grab lunch during the ten minutes I had before the producer lost her mind trying to find me. As I walked down the street, I passed a man with no arms or legs, with a cardboard sign begging for help.

I've been on radio shows where I've gotten a lot of flak for advocating giving homeless people a dollar when you see them on the street. Many people think the homeless are an eyesore. Critics say, "Let them go get a job, head for a shelter. Whatever they do, make them just stop bugging me on the street! Besides, if I give them something, they're going to abuse it, right? They'll just buy more booze."

Yet even so, I try, not always successfully, to always give a dollar to someone who puts his hand out on the street. My reasoning is that this act grants the homeless person a moment of dignity. I put a dollar in his hand and say, "God bless you, sir." And it's worth the buck just to hear him say it back, "God bless you, too, sir. God bless you, too." I know that He is listening to that exchange. I know that I have been a blessing to this fallen human brother for just a moment.

Think about it: what a bargain! For one dollar, you can bestow dignity on another human being. And in this situation, even though I was late, hungry, and completely stressed out, I did stop and hand over a dollar to the man with no arms or legs.

It doesn't always happen that way. Occasionally, I am in a rotten mood. There are problems in the office, or I just came from a meeting where someone I am dependent on turned down a deal I was counting on. Whatever the case, my heart is closed, and I don't make enough of an effort to open it. I justify walking right past a person in need because I am focused on my own pain, rather than on his. And I lose the opportunity to be a blessing. What a waste! All for one measly buck.

That's the struggle of being a blessing, in a nutshell. It's easy 99 percent of the time to do the right thing, but being a true blessing also entails struggling to do the right thing that extra 1 percent of the time.

Another time, I was flying to L.A. On the plane a few rows in front of me, I saw a husband and a wife, clearly full of affection for each other. I couldn't help but notice how considerate they were, helping each other out, clearly interested in what the other had to say. They were a beautiful couple and so in love. As I watched them, it struck me that my wife is kind to me in that very same way. It filled my heart with love, and I wanted to pick up the phone, on the spur of the moment, and call her to say, *"You're the greatest wife."*

I tried to hang on to the impulse, but by the time I was in L.A., hours later, my mood had changed. I wanted to get to my hotel, get settled, figure out my schedule for the trip; where earlier I had felt warmth and kindness, now all I felt was pressure.

I noticed how my emotions had changed. I no longer felt like calling my wife and giving her the compliment because, after all, we had so many practical things to discuss. There was no time for romance. Then it hit me: the part of me that wants to bless others— that's the true me! The other part, the stressed part, is what I need to overcome. So I called up my wife and said what I had meant to say from the beginning. I told her how much I love her and how glad she makes me every day. It put me in a better mood. The pressures eased a little. Don't let another day go by in which you are a burden to the person who loves you the most. Consult with your inner voice of conscience and resolve, in self-talk, to be a blessing to your spouse. Say,

In my marriage I want to be much more romantic, because being a blessing to someone who has given up everyone and everything else to be with me means lifting his/her burden through romantic gestures. Without romance, a marriage becomes pure drudgery. And that's quite a burden.

I'm committing to make three important romantic gestures a week—such as buying a small gift, taking my spouse out on a date, and writing him/her a romantic e-mail—and then two smaller, daily romantic gestures, such as giving simple compliments and signs of my appreciation. After all, is it really so hard to tell my wife I appreciate that my shirts are always pressed? Is it really that difficult to tell my husband I appreciate that he changes the lightbulbs around the house?

Being a blessing in marriage also means giving my spouse sexual pleasure. The selfish lover is a tremendous burden. He/she makes the other person feel as if he/she is used for sex and certainly not as if they are making love. Intense sexual pleasure with the person I love is such an incredible blessing. It has the power to wash away the accumulated burdens and pressures of the day. And I don't want to deny this to my spouse.

I want to help my spouse feel free and unburdened. I want him/her to feel calm and serene. I'm going to push myself to massage my spouse's shoulders, back, legs, and then move on to more erogenous areas. I'll refrain from simply indulging in my own pleasure and leaving my spouse unsatisfied, because I want to be a romantic, sexual, and erotic blessing to my marriage and my spouse.

Don't stop there. Extend the gesture to the rest of your life. Say to yourself,

I want to be a blessing not only to my family but also to complete strangers, to people who can't do anything for me in return. Because that's the biggest test of whether I'm serious about this or not.

I'm going to start saying "Hello" and "How are you doing?" to strangers I meet in elevators when I get in, instead of just staring ahead and pretending that they're invisible. I'm not looking for any deep conversation, and I don't want to make people feel uncomfortable. Rather, I want them to feel as if they are present and that I acknowledge them.

When I get into a cab, rather than jumping right onto the phone or staring out the window, I'll get into a short, pleasant conversation, asking the driver where he's from and how his day is going. I recognize that so many of the drivers are immigrants to this country, and I never want to convey any feeling that I condescend to them or that I think they exist only to take me from point A to B. I want to acknowledge their uniqueness, be polite, and serve as a blessing that way.

I'm going to sit my kids down and tell them that this is how we treat all people. We're polite and courteous not only to our friends but also to those who do jobs that aren't always appreciated. This means that they should go over to the gardener and offer him a cold drink. They should thank the cleaning woman for her hard work and ask if she needs anything. It also means that we as a family will invite her and her family to our home for dinner every few months to show them that we acknowledge their humanity.

Finally, I want to be a blessing to God, the source of all blessing. It's His world. He put me on this earth to visit sick people in the hospital and to offer comfort at funerals and houses of mourning—to invite people into my home and offer hospitality, just as God offers me and my family constant hospitality in this beautiful world He has blessed us with.

I can do it. I face these choices every day, and from now on, I will always choose to be a blessing.

We all walk around saddled by the fear that we're insignificant. Yet every one of us has the chance to lessen that burden for another person. Be a blessing, and seize your opportunity to improve someone else's life.

To develop a personalized relationship with your inner voice of conscience, ask yourself the following questions. Respond to them, and let the answers guide you on self-talks of your own devising.

Do I harbor resentment against members of my family? Am I estranged from any of my siblings or cousins? Have my relationships with friends gone off course?

When I hear people arguing, do I try to make peace, or do I throw fuel on the fire?

Do I have a good relationship with my kids? Do I expect them always to apologize to me because I am the parent, or do I accept that I, too, have flaws?

Do I maintain a positive relationship with my coworkers? And if I come under a great deal of pressure, do I apologize for my shortness of tone and careless remarks?

In the end, does my voice of conscience remind me at all times to choose to be a blessing, or do I carelessly burden my fellow man?

PART III

The Voice of
the Innermost Self

8

Seek to Struggle

CONVERSATION 8

I will teach myself to wrestle with great moral issues and life's struggles and to persevere in the face of difficulty.

I have at times been envious of those for whom life seems to come easy. I envied their sunny personalities, charm, and social adroitness. And I'm not just talking about trust-fund babies who never had to worry about paying their college tuition or mortgage. I also mean people who were born with everything they needed to succeed—either natural beauty, a calm nature, or an innate ability to impress. Some people seem to have a natural grace that smoothes their way with others, though they barely make an effort. I have never had that gift.

I am not one of those lucky people. For me, good things come only with struggle. To be sure, God has been extraordinarily kind to me. Although I was raised in a home where money was tight, we always had food to eat and a roof over our heads. I am very grateful for all of my blessings. But I have always had to wrestle with myself to master my emotions. I have always had an impulsive and unpredictable nature. Although I sometimes feel down, I don't, thank God, get depressed, and I am blessed with energy. Yet for me, optimism is an uphill battle, and happiness is a serious challenge.

I am fortunate, thank God, to have a very loving and devoted wife. Much of what is good and settled about my life is due to my wife's exemplary and highly giving nature. Supporting my family has always been a challenge. We have had good years, yes, but then there were more difficult years. In general, the financial security that should have by now accrued to someone who has worked hard for twenty-five years to support a large family has yet to happen.

Then there is my role as parent. I have nine wonderful children, but raising them has never been easy. On the contrary, my children all have strong, individualistic personalities (although I sometimes can't help but wonder, couldn't a few of them be uncomplicated like their mother?). I have had to find the balance between wanting to sculpt them in my image and accepting that I must give them the latitude to grow and develop themselves. I have also sought to minimize volatility in their lives so that they can grow to be much more stable and settled than their father has been.

I tell you all of this because, my blessings notwithstanding, my path has always been marked by struggle. And that struggle has made all the difference in my life.

I suspect that you, too, must contend with personal difficulties. If you didn't, you probably wouldn't be reading this book. But get this: I'm not here to change you. Nor will I help you make your struggles go away. This conversation will not give you a magic potion to drink that will turn you into someone charming, beautiful, or successful. On the contrary, *this conversation is all about the virtue of struggle.*

Engage in self-talk with the voice of your inner self, authenticity, and truest essence. It will admit the truth about struggle. Say to yourself,

> I've always wanted things to be easy. I wanted so badly for my many struggles to be resolved. I wanted my life at work to be easy.

I hoped to sail through the promotion process, earning more and more money and living the American dream. I wanted to buy whatever I wanted and not have to worry about whether I could afford it.

I've always wanted kids who listened to everything I said. Kids who would get up in the morning, make their beds, go to school and pay attention in class, come home, do the yard work for me, do their homework, have dinner with their parents, and go to bed on their own.

I wanted a marriage that I didn't have to work on, where my wife and I always felt passionately attracted to each other. I wanted us to have great sex every night without really trying—a fiery connection that never dissipated.

But I have to be honest. *I care about things only when I really struggle and fight for them.*

People are like olives, the Talmud says. You get the oil only when they're pressed. These struggles that we face every day are no burden but a blessing, even if they don't feel like it at the time. To understand why, you must engage with your inner voice every day and in your conversations find goodness in the struggle. As hard as it is, you must battle against your emotions, financial constraints, and marital difficulties and at long last against the constraints of aging and life itself. The reason?

Only through struggle does life become meaningful.

In this country, our goal is supposed to be to "make it." None of our heroes has to struggle, so why should we? The American dream is to reach a stage where struggle is a thing of the past—to *arrive*, as they say. After that, you can take it easy and sit around basking in the adulation of the have-nots, all of whom are still struggling to get to where you are.

All politicians speak about how they struggled and then finally arrived. They get up at their big political conventions and reel off predictable speeches. "When I was a boy, our family was so poor that I had to steal oats from the hogs to survive. The clothing I wore to school was stitched together from discarded corn husks. We lived inside a giant old tractor tire, and instead of Play-Doh, we were forced to make toys out of earwax. Mom worked as a coffee-bean crusher for Starbucks, and Dad, when he wasn't drinking or womanizing, worked as a human tester for experimental drugs. When I was ten, my uncle Rufus stole one of my kidneys to support his crystal meth habit. Things hit rock bottom when we were forced to eat my pet hamster Tinkerbell for Thanksgiving. Dad carved the poor little thing into a feast for ten." From there, they go on to tell us how hard work brought them to the pinnacle where they are today, which is begging for your votes. Wild applause. "My struggle is over at last." And, so they say, it can be for you as well, as long as you make them your mayor or governor or so-and-so.

This delusional approach to struggle doesn't apply only to today's political leaders. Just look at all of the lies we are told about our country's founders. If you believe what they teach you in grade school, George Washington never had to struggle to be a good person. It came naturally to him. He cut down a cherry tree and then instantly confessed to it because he could never tell a lie. And Abraham Lincoln—here's a man who was practically superhuman. He trekked across the Serengeti plains and the Sahara Desert to return a single penny to a store owner who had overpaid him, all because he was a paragon of truthfulness and hard work. These heroes never had to struggle: they always rose above difficult circumstances—life for them was a breeze.

It should come as no surprise that all of this is pure balderdash. If you look at the facts, nothing was easy for these men—they had to struggle to make it, just as the rest of us do. Their goodness came only after terrific exertion. As we later learned from biographers such as Joseph Ellis, Washington was a social climber who married the richest widow in Virginia. And Lincoln, as great a man as he was, was so depressed most of the time that his friends kept sharp knives away from him. Once upon a time we looked at Martin Luther King

Jr. as a perfect saint. Now we know that he was human and had to struggle to be faithful in his marriage.

Thank God that we know the truth about our heroes. It doesn't lessen their stature at all. Now that we see how they had to struggle, the adversity they had to face, these men can truly inspire us. After all, without struggle, what would make someone into a hero?

If we seek to struggle in our lives, we need palpable, comprehensible heroes. Dismiss from your life the false heroes who feign perfection. Choose instead the heroes with flaws, those who had to struggle to overcome difficulties. Begin with your parents.

My father is like me, a complicated man, but his struggles were far, far greater than mine. As a young boy in Iran, he was truly destitute. He lived in a tent with thirteen siblings and then left with his family in the 1950s to come to Israel when Israel was little more than sand. There's a picture of him in his school in Iran. Every kid there is dressed in clothing that is so patched up, it is no longer made of any material at all, it's just a collection of patches. He didn't have shoes. His shoes were made of rubber cut out of discarded tires. (No, I'm not making this up. Nor am I running for office, at least not yet.)

Now, this is not your run-of-the-mill rags-to-riches story. He did rise from poverty to build a business, thank God, but that's not the point. The point is that after being robbed of a childhood and having to go to work from about age ten, he had to learn to toughen up. He thus, understandably, found it difficult to show emotion and vulnerability. How could he show weakness when so many mouths depended on him?

At the time of my parents' divorce, we lived in L.A. My mother decided to move us to Miami, where her parents and brother lived and where she would have her family's support. At the time, I didn't think my father even minded. I was eight years old, we were leaving, and I didn't see it bothering him. What could I know of my father's emotions? Only a few years later did I hear from a rabbi I got to know in L.A. that he used to invite my father over for Sabbath dinner. My father, he told me, would sit at the dinner table and cry over his separation from his children.

What I respect so much about my father is that he wrestled with his emotions to become more emotionally available. For the first few years of my life, he found it challenging to tell me he loved me. It wasn't easy for a man such as him, who had suffered through a very hard life, to say something like that. But then, by and by, after years of struggle, his emotions poured forth. Today he is the adored grandfather of my children, whom he hugs and kisses. They revere him and find him the most interesting grandfather in the world. He is a very rugged Middle Eastern man who survived by his wits. My friends call him leathery. When you come from a background and an upbringing like that, you don't show vulnerability, you don't show emotion. But he did, and I knew that it came amid phenomenal struggle.

My mother has also been a tremendous inspiration to me during my life. She had an unhappy marriage and, after the divorce, five kids to raise on her own. She worked two jobs to put us through private Jewish day school so we could learn about our tradition. She spent the day as a bank teller, went straight home, made dinner, and then went to another job. That's what she did for years to support her kids. It was a Herculean struggle to triumph over these many challenges, yet she raised her kids with solid values. And unlike others who struggle and become bitter, my mother is one of the most gracious and loving people you will ever meet.

For many people, parents are the first and best role models you have—especially once you have children of your own. Even if you had disagreements, even if you blame them for their legitimate mistakes, they're still the only parents you will get. Sometimes it takes decades for people to forgive their parents or to understand where they were coming from. But when I realized that I had much to learn from my parents' struggle, it was life changing.

I remember the self-talk well. It was late at night, and everyone in the house except me was asleep. I said to myself,

Once upon a time I promised myself that I would never repeat my parents' mistakes. Whenever my parents bickered in front of me, I swore to myself that I would never do that to my children. I told myself that I would always model constructive, loving, positive behavior. I would be respectful to my spouse in front of my kids, never criticize without showering my children with compliments, and always work to give them a happy childhood.

Back then I told myself that every day would be like Disneyland, but now that my nine children have arrived, I'm starting to understand just how hard my parents were working after all.

It's more challenging to raise children than I ever imagined. Kids never listen as much as they should, and no matter how much we parents do, we never feel completely appreciated. Sometimes it seems as if my kids are more interested in being around their friends than around me. It hurts me, and I feel as if I don't know their secrets. So, what happened?

My mistake was to dismiss my own parents' struggle.

Now I see my parents in a whole new heroic light. Their errors, though significant, are utterly subordinate to the devotion they showed me. My gosh, it wasn't easy for them. And it's not easy for me, either. The fact that I'm prepared to engage in that struggle means I'm prepared to be heroic the way my parents were before me.

I suspect that one of the most difficult issues for people who live a life touched by struggle is the lack of role models. After all, whom do we have to look to besides our parents? America's celebrity-driven culture has few legitimately admirable people for us to admire—and I've already discussed politicians. I was raised with the Jewish understanding of righteousness. According to that philosophy, we struggle to do right despite our predilection to do otherwise. In the Jewish Bible, there isn't a single perfect person. Each is flawed. Every one of them had to struggle. They all had crises of faith. As a result, the conviction that we have to fight for what is right was instilled in me from an early age.

This is not so for a number of Christians. Many of my Christian friends have lapsed in the observance of their faith. One principal reason, I believe, is many Christians' insistence on the absolute perfection of Jesus. Many in the church believe that Jesus has too often been utterly stripped of his humanity, even though classical Christian theology emphasizes that Jesus was both fully divine and fully human. Even if you accept that Jesus was the Son of God, a perfect and angelic creation, where is the fully human part?

A perfect, nonhuman Christ cannot fully touch the lives of ordinary Christians. We can't relate to perfect people, because we are not, despite our best intentions, angels. Somebody as perfect as Jesus, someone so divine, can't possibly understand our worldly struggles. Success and the right choices come naturally to him but not to the rest of us.

To all of my Christian readers, I suggest that you ask yourself what Jesus *the man* must have struggled with. You have to identify with the stories and themes of your own religion if they are to be useful as you take on the struggles of your own life.

Times are hard for many Americans, as far as money is concerned. So many of us today are struggling with financial difficulties. There's never enough money, our bosses ask us to work harder for less pay, and a raise always seems to be out of the question—if we're not already on the cusp of being laid off. So many people I speak to in counseling are grappling with these difficulties—especially those who are working in jobs for love and not money.

Barry is one of those people. An airline pilot, he found himself sacrificing a great deal just to continue working in the profession he loved. "My financial situation is killing me," Barry said. "I love flying, but I'm just not earning enough money." He had five children, with three already in college, on a pilot's salary (which is not generous). On top of that, his work requires him to be away from home for long stretches. "The thing that really kills me is that I have to spend so much time away from home, and yet I'm *still* in a financial hole.

"It's all starting to eat away at me," he said. "I'm beginning to resent my own children for wanting to go to good colleges, and I find it hard to look at myself in the mirror, since I can't seem to solve this mess on my own. What can I possibly do now?"

I was at a loss. I'm no financial planner, and I told him so. "While I can't tell you how to dig yourself out of this hole, the one thing you can always control is how you react. Remind yourself that major airlines trust you and put the lives of hundreds of people in your hands every day. You are a remarkable man, and that's what your colleagues, your wife, and your kids see, every day.

"Regarding your financial difficulties—I'll have to defer to the far more competent advisers who can help you weather the storm. Yet I can tell you this: the reason you became despondent is because *you expected not to struggle*. You thought things would always improve, but that's not the way life is. Embrace the struggle. Think through your options. Necessity is the mother of invention. It will work out and you'll be a stronger, more determined, and more inspiring man."

Barry's story is all too common. So many others have to face the difficulty of doing the thing they love, yet not making enough money in spite of it. I urge people in this situation to take heart. Speak truly to the inner voice of your truest self, and remind yourself,

> What I do for a living is absolutely vital, *but it will always be a struggle for me to do what I love.* All that I can do is draw strength from the struggle. I grasp that my struggle is precisely what imparts meaning to my life. It reasserts my love for what I am doing just to know that.

I have my own experiences with financial struggle. Debbie and I got married in Sydney, Australia, in 1988 and had to use the money we'd gotten as wedding gifts to buy tickets back to the United States. In our first year of living in New York, I was studying to be a rabbi. We survived because Debbie was earning $200 a week separating big clumps of jewelry that had been returned from department stores (yes, there is a job like that). When Debbie got pregnant with our first child, she was feeling ill and had to give up the job. We now had no money at all. I used to come home from a long day of study, put my head between my hands, and wonder how we would pay the rent.

Yet unexpected blessings often arise from struggle. It was because of this crisis that I started to write. I had an idea for a book about dream interpretation. A small publisher offered me $250 a week over a few months to write the book. That money saved us. Every day, when I came home after a long day of studying for my rabbinical exams, I ate dinner with my wife for half an hour and then immediately went to the computer to work on writing the book.

In the meantime, many of my colleagues from the yeshiva were being supported by their parents and in-laws, which was the custom. They had no worries about paying rent. They did not have to struggle. I remember one friend in particular who lived in a beautiful spare apartment that belonged to his parents. While I was struggling to make the rent, he seemed to have money to burn. Yet because I had to write, you're reading my words right now. *Dreams: Deciphering Our Visions of the Night* was my first book. This is my twenty-fifth, thank God, and it all started because we struggled. And the friend who was on his parents' very generous dole? He remains that way up to the present, having entered the family business, where he still works today. Even now, he has no money worries.

I continue to have them. Twenty-five books. An impressive achievement, I hope. But many have sold only twenty-five copies. And with nine children in Jewish day schools so that they can learn about their ancient faith, money is still hard to come by.

Like you, I have had to earn whatever I have. I never achieved wealth. I wish I had. Honestly. But I also know there is even greater virtue in having to wrestle to support my family, put my kids through college, and keep a roof over their heads. For my children, who witness the daily struggle, it is a mark of my infinite love. They know how much they mean to me because they see how hard I work to support them. They know that for me, supporting the family is the most important thing of all, even—and especially—because it is a struggle.

So when I speak to myself about my situation, I can say whole-heartedly, "I know people for whom life is a lot easier. I know people who come from moneyed backgrounds. They don't have to worry, as I do, about paying their bills. Their parents will always help them. Or maybe they caught a lucky break and got into a great investment at the right time. But although I, like anyone, want financial security, I would not trade places with any of these people.

"Just as I'm proud of my life and of my family, I'm proud of my struggles. By struggling, I prove myself a better person every day, and above all else I value the opportunity to test myself against a worthy cause."

There are few struggles as difficult as achieving a happy marriage. Most people fail at it these days. One principal reason is that they're willing to work from nine to five, practically killing themselves when they're in the office, but they refuse to do any further work on their lives when they're at home. Where did the notion that marriages don't require work come from? M. Scott Peck once wrote, "Love is not a feeling. Love is an action, an activity." This is absolutely right.

Love is a willingness to nurture the spiritual growth of another.
Love is a verb. It demands endeavor.

Yet we continue to embrace Hollywood's empty definition of love, where romance happens automatically and arbitrarily, as effortlessly as a magic spell. What you never see is a love story that requires hard work. Nor are we ever treated to an accurate depiction of what happens to marriages when no one does that work: bitterness steadily accrues, until the two partners can barely stand each other.

How does this come about? A lot of men define themselves as problem solvers, so over time they naturally begin to consider their wives weak or less effective than they are. "Why can't you do what I do?" they ask at every opportunity. "I told you we're running late;

why aren't you driving more aggressively?" Women also tend to act in safer ways, so this is another reason husbands may think of them as weak. "What do you mean, the kids don't listen to you? You're not a strong enough disciplinarian, and you let the kids step all over you." At the same time, a husband like this begins to feel that every problem is his to solve. Disciplining the kids, supporting the family, fixing the car, it's all exclusively his responsibility.

It's a short hop from those feelings into far uglier territory, where husbands dismiss their wives as being outright stupid. "Oh," they'll say, "I love my wife, but she's not really that bright." I hear this all of the time from men—it's so insulting, so arrogant and thoughtless.

Wives have a parallel approach. They begin to believe that *they* are the only ones who do anything. "You don't do anything around the house, you don't listen when I speak to you; the only time you're interested in me is at night when it's time for sex. Suddenly, you're attentive, you're loving—but I'm not a light switch. You can't press the On button whenever you want me to be romantic with you for four minutes." That bitterness becomes even more heightened when wives feel that their husbands are not focused on them.

Karl and Gail came to me for counseling. Karl was not a very emotional guy. A man of few words, he was nonetheless excellent at getting things done and was a very practical and focused person. His problem? He had no compunction about saying to me in front of his wife, "You know, I have to do everything for our household, because my wife just isn't capable. She's simply not very bright."

Karl was doing a great deal wrong. He rarely said anything affectionate to Gail. Every day he came home and belittled his wife, asking, "What did you do today? While I did all of this work, what did you do at home?" He was dismissive of her responsibilities. She would be at home taking care of two toddlers, and he would make fun of her, asking, "How long does that take, an hour?"

Conversely, she could get also very negative. She was starved for affection in her marriage. There was nothing she could do to get real love. Her husband never realized during these counseling sessions just how much he put her down.

Keeping this marriage together would be a struggle for both of them. Karl would have to overcome his nature to stop insulting his wife. Gail, on the other hand, had to wrestle with her own negativity. She said so many times, "Why are you telling me not to be negative? Look at my life. I'm trapped in this awful marriage. Why shouldn't I be negative?"

I said to her, "You seem to be saying that you cannot control your moods and that you're utterly controlled by other people. If that's the case, then you're not the master of your own life. No one can make you negative unless you choose to be negative. No one can make you into something you don't want to be. If it is a struggle to be otherwise, then that is a struggle you must seek out, first and foremost, because *marriage will always be a struggle.*"

Truly, it is never easy to maintain your relationship with your spouse. Love is not a dead organism that you conquer and settle. It is a living, breathing thing, and it will always take effort. Struggle is central to a marriage, just as it is central to all other dimensions of life. The fact that love requires work is a demonstration of how much your beloved means to you. If you aren't prepared to fight for something, then you don't care about it.

The toughest struggle of any marriage will inevitably be to maintain an erotic connection. Sexual desire results from many things. The desire for intimacy is the first source, as I have discussed, and the procreative urge is also a large part of it. Certain other ingredients are essential for sexual desire, though. Novelty is undoubtedly one of them. Novelty is the spice of life. Take newness out of something, and you've ensured that it will be predictable, routine, and boring.

Who would ever expect that you could live with the same person, day in and day out, and still make love to him or her, year after year? Where's the novelty in that? Yet in American society, all of the sexual taboos have been thrown out except for three: adultery, incest, and pedophilia. If you cheat on your wife, you're a social pariah. You won't be elected president; you may even be impeached for it.

Some would argue that that hardly seems fair. Every evolutionary biologist will tell us that it's natural to seek many sexual partners. The result is that you see two kinds of marriages.

The first, and most common, is where the couple simply accepts that sex will eventually taper off. Statistics show that one in three marriages is loveless, sexually platonic. Even young couples are having sex only once a week for, at best, ten minutes at a time, which is the national average.

What this means is that America has accepted that being lovers in marriage is not really doable. Instead, we've invented this awful term: *best friend*. "Here's my wife," we'll say. "She's my best friend." We would *never* have used that expression a hundred years ago—it would have been an insult. Best friend—really? That's all? You're going to use such a casual and demeaning term to describe the most important relationship in your life?

Fortunately, there is a second kind of couple. These couples refuse to go quietly into that dark night. They choose to fight—their love is simply too special to give up. They understand that sexuality is the soul of a relationship, and if they're not carnally intimate, if they don't press closely to each other, then they can't call themselves soul mates.

I maintain that the termination of the couple's sex life is a functional termination of the marriage itself. It really is a struggle to stay sexually connected, and I'll be the first to admit that this sounds unsexy. Such is the flickering nature of erotic love.

Those who choose not to struggle with sexual desire pay the price in unexpected ways. John F. Kennedy did not wrestle much with keeping the sex good in his marriage. It's been reported that he would simply go to another woman whenever he got bored. All of his mistresses who wrote memoirs agreed on one thing: he was terrible in bed. The reason is pretty obvious, if you think about it. If he ever felt even the slightest pang of a struggle, he went straight to another woman. The result? He had no technique; he didn't know how to expand his sexual repertoire in order to please a woman. The fireworks that men and women create happen only because they bring novelty to the relationship, not by finding another partner but by having an erotic conversation or by employing all five senses with the person they're committed to.

JFK lacked all of that. When a man doesn't need to discover something novel in a woman because he simply exchanges one woman for another, he will never learn about a woman's erotic mind.

When you feel the strain of your relationship, admit it to yourself. When you are angry or annoyed, or even when you feel tired of dealing with your spouse, listen to the voice of your inner self and engage yourself in honest self-talk by saying,

> I don't feel as attracted to my spouse as I once was, and I'm sorry to say that I think he/she feels the same way about me. I don't see my spouse looking at me when I change clothes or walk around the bedroom naked. I can be taking a shower, and he/she doesn't even pay attention. Truth be told, I sometimes feel more attracted to some of my coworkers in the office or even complete strangers I see on the street than to my spouse. I'm kind of embarrassed to admit it, but I even think about some of these people when I'm having sex with my spouse. It's the only way I can get truly aroused. The personal, intimate connection is simply absent. It will now be my struggle to rekindle that connection.

There isn't a marriage on earth that's free of struggle. The struggles with boredom and with keeping the spark alive are the most common of all. They are crucial opportunities for us to rise above, become better people, and deepen our relationships. As difficult as they may be, imagine if your marriage were haunted by worse struggles?

When I was rabbi to the students of Oxford, a young man named Henry was studying history there. He remains a very close friend of mine to this day. Henry called me up one night in tears and told me that a terrible thing had happened: his father had passed away. As more information came in, the news became worse: it turned out his father hadn't just passed away peacefully, he had taken his own life. His marriage, some years later, was complicated by his emotional turmoil. I remember his wife, Heidi, coming to me and saying, "I didn't sign up for this. I know he lost his father, and that's a tragedy. But the ghost of his father is haunting our marriage."

I had to explain to Heidi a strange but very real phenomenon—by confronting this tragedy, her husband was showing true greatness. I told her, "How can you demonstrate true love if you're not prepared to struggle to love someone who has endured phenomenal pain? On the contrary, it's what makes your existence necessary. You have the great blessing in marriage of not only being loved by a husband but being needed as well.

"Every day, your husband is telling you that he *really* needs you, he doesn't merely love you. He's saying, 'I'm facing tremendous pain, but our relationship makes it all make sense. It can be burdensome, I know, but I still need you.' Consult with the voice of your inner self, and you will understand the situation even more fully. 'True love is imperfect,' you should tell yourself. 'Even when I love someone fully, I still find myself attracted to strangers. And why is that? Because it is a struggle to love the same person endlessly.' Every day that you join in that struggle, you're choosing your spouse anew. If you fell in love with someone and were never attracted to anyone else, you'd become complacent. But when you need to choose your husband anew, you recommit to him on a daily basis. *That's why struggle is so precious.* That's why you need to fight to save your relationship every single day."

One of the last and most intense struggles of our lives is our battle against time. We all accept, quite rightly, that a certain amount of bodily decline is inevitable. Problems begin to arise, however, when we start to believe that the world belongs to the young. As if once we're past fifty, we're done—and if we get much older than that, we might as well be shipped off to a nursing home, lest we get in all of the young people's way.

I reject this phenomenon completely. As of the writing of this book, I'm in my midforties. When I was a young man, I always enjoyed cycling but never took it seriously as a form of exercise. Now, I can't get enough of it. Yesterday I took a thirty-mile ride; the day before that, I rode for twenty miles. I truly enjoy this activity, but the strangest thing is that when I was in my twenties, I didn't have the willpower to exert myself this way. Now that I am more mature, I can struggle against the inertia of age and do something truly youthful.

King Solomon said that his youth was his winter, and his old age was his summer. That runs contrary to how we see age in this country. Olympic athletes are considered old and used up by the time they are age twenty-five—these people are supposed to be in the winter of their lives? Yet King Solomon was right: he meant that when he was young, he was stupid and made so many mistakes. When he got older, he knew right from wrong, and that was the time to breathe free.

To be blunt, although it is acceptable for a person to struggle with weight issues, people in the United States don't seem to think that we need to struggle with age. Nevertheless, it's truly important to remain active, to try new things, and to be joyous even as you age. What authority said that age forty, fifty, sixty, or even seventy is old? If life is important to us, then we must struggle to hang onto it. And if our bodies throw new aches and pains at us, then let that be part of the struggle as well. As with all other things, it is the struggle that proves something is meaningful, and age is no exception.

Every time you feel that you are too old, too tired, or unwilling to try something new, engage the voice of your inner self in serious and direct self-talk and say,

> I need to struggle against age. I need to oppose the inertia that seems so much a part of my life. I need to do new things and take advantage of all that life has to offer, especially activities I may not even have been able to do when I was younger. There is no limit to what I can do—and all the better if it's a struggle for me at first. *The struggle is what gives my life meaning.*

. . .

Why is struggle so important? Because it is the last and greatest test of heroism that we have.

I believe that every single person wants to be a hero. Nobody believes he or she is ordinary. Everyone thinks he or she is cut out for something extraordinary—and this doesn't necessarily mean being elected president. It means we want to be heroic to ourselves and to other people in our everyday lives, even if it's hard—*especially* if it's hard.

If you struggle with a great obstacle in life and you triumph, then, voilà! You're a hero. If you fight to feed your family, put your kids through college, keep a roof over their heads, seek out struggle, and triumph, then you are a hero, nothing less.

Perhaps you stayed married when all of your friends got divorced. Or maybe you got divorced after all but continued to believe in love, triumphing over cynicism. You engaged in a struggle, and you were victorious. There is no greater accomplishment in life than that.

Heroism results when the good is pitted against the not-so-good, and the good triumphs. We all want that in our lives. Every time I lose my temper with my kids, I've lost. I'm not a hero. Conversely, when I resist that urge to get upset and instead control myself, even that little victory is a form of heroics.

We all believe we were born for some heroic struggle. It could be the person who fights for animal rights, the one who tries to save the environment, or the individual who advocates for children—all see themselves as heroes.

Heroism speaks to the human desire to be extraordinary, and it involves a never-ending struggle with new difficulties every single day. Lincoln was our greatest president, and what was the reason? He faced a conflict that was nowhere near as clear-cut as the one that George Washington led. The South *did* enslave people, which is undoubtedly evil. But the Civil War was also seen as a matter of states' rights—who was Lincoln to tell people how to live? He was called an autocrat and a tyrant, and he had to struggle against that, too.

For us everyday heroes-in-the-making, sometimes it may seem as though life is too hard and the struggle is too much. Yet those who feel as if they are cursed with heavy burdens, with the task of raising children alone, being married to a complicated spouse, or coping with a complex upbringing—they are the chosen few. Life will always be harder for them. They may receive little appreciation, but they are the great ones. They are the ones who demonstrate to the world that certain things are so precious, they're worth fighting for.

Say to yourself,

> I have experienced the ecstasy of achieving small victories after struggling and working hard to succeed. It's never been easy for me, but I have never retreated from the battle, either. And in the process it has built tremendous character in me.
>
> I now understand that anything in life that you don't struggle for is not very valuable. That's why Herculean efforts are required for all of the achievements I listed previously: supporting my family, raising my kids, keeping my marriage fresh, and overcoming my sour moods. To struggle means that I'm alive, I'm engaged, I'm involved, and I'm invested. I understand that this is how I become a hero to my children, by showing them that I never quit—that certain tasks are so precious to me that I don't ever retreat from them. I never tire of working on them because they are life's most precious duties.

We need to embrace struggle and stop complaining about our lives. The absence of struggle is no virtue. We should treasure our little challenges and trials, because they make us into the best people we can be.

To develop a personalized relationship with the voice of your innermost self, ask yourself the following questions. Respond to them, and let the answers guide you on self-talks of your own devising.

Do I punish myself whenever I fail? Am I always self-critical so that I forget the need to pick myself up by the bootstraps when I fall?

When my kids fail at something or when my spouse feels down and depressed, do I indulge in self-pity with them, or do I teach them how to pick themselves up?

When I have financial setbacks, do I get morbid and dispirited, or do I understand that things will improve in time?

Do I consult my inner voice of inspiration every day, so that when I set my mind to something and struggle with it, I know that it will eventually yield?

When I feel let down by God because something sad or tragic has befallen me, do I simply abandon the relationship altogether and shun God, or do I live up to the word "Israel," which means "he who wrestles with God"?

9

Always Ask

I recognize that life is about wrestling with great questions, yet I know full well that there are no ultimate solutions.

Because I have devoted much of my time to rescuing families and saving marriages, people often ask me what I believe to be the most important ingredient of a successful relationship. They expect me to reel off vague, clichéd answers such as communication, trust, or romance. My response often surprises them: curiosity.

The soul of every relationship is curiosity. As long as you are curious about your significant other, wanting to know his or her mind, heart, and spirit, you will always lean in toward the person, take an interest, build closeness, and make him or her feel special. But as curiosity ebbs, relationships die. Once you think you know everything and that there's nothing left to discover, there is no need to explore further. Your marriage is no longer a journey but a destination. You've already arrived. Boredom sets in. To keep life interesting, you sometimes look for someone outside the relationship, a new person to explore. Either way, you've fallen out of love and are unable to deepen the connection you once had.

Only curiosity can resurrect a relationship. If you keep asking questions, you'll spend your lives on a mutual journey of discovery, always wanting to know more. Your relationship will become inexhaustible. Not only that, if you can apply that same curiosity to the rest of your life, you'll find no end to the benefits of asking questions.

The good life is one in which you always seek to know, whereas the stultifying life is when you think you already know.

There are, as always, two kinds of people. One type believes that the more they live, the more they know. Life acquires a been-there-done-that quality. For new stimulation, they either immerse themselves in a world of make-believe via movies, TV, and the Internet, or they push the envelope to find extremes. This is where extravagant spending, drugs, affairs, and extreme sports come in, with the latter being the least damaging as long as one is safe.

The other kind of person believes precisely the opposite. This type thinks that the more they live, the more they discover how infinitely complex God, life, and people are and the more ignorant they feel. I don't say this with false humility, but I am firmly in the latter camp. I have published twenty-five books, thank God, but I am amazed at how little I still know. Relationships continue to flummox me. The more I study them, the more mysterious they become. I once believed that I was an expert in child rearing, but life humbles you, as do teenagers. Every year, as a religious Jew, I read the Bible from cover to cover. Sometimes I wonder, "Why am I doing this? I already know what it says." Yet as I go through the cycle, I am blown away by newer, deeper levels of mystery and meaning that show me that I have just scratched the surface.

When the philosopher Socrates was told that the oracle at Delphi had identified him as the wisest person in all of Greece, he reportedly smiled and said, "If that is so, it is only because I alone know that I don't know." Similarly, the Zohar, the main book of the Kabbalah, says, "The pinnacle of knowledge about God is to know what we cannot know."

Think of the most interesting people you've met. Were they pedantic windbags who thought they knew it all? Not a chance—a person who only *answers* questions, never asking, comes across as an arrogant, tiresome bore.

The truly fascinating people are those who constantly ask.

When I was a rabbi at Oxford University, I was privileged to enjoy a warm friendship with Sir Isaiah Berlin, regarded as one of the greatest and most erudite thinkers of the twentieth century. Twice a year, I would bring a group of Rhodes scholars to meet the great philosopher, then in his nineties.

On one occasion, in conversation, a certain student windbag who was trying to impress Sir Isaiah that he was a walking encyclopedia quoted the philosopher Martin Heidegger. We were all startled when Sir Isaiah said, "Oh, I've never really read him. Perhaps you can come over and teach me about some of his ideas when you have time." Here was one of the most esteemed intellectuals on earth admitting he didn't know something and asking a student to teach him. Was he serious? We were in awe at his humility. It was a sign of Sir Isaiah's insatiable thirst for knowledge. He had nothing to prove. He just wanted to know. After all, what had made him such a great thinker was his infinite curiosity.

Finding an inspiration such as Sir Isaiah Berlin is challenging in contemporary America. For us, curiosity is a rarity. Turn on the cable news channels or listen to talk radio and you'll see that everyone already knows everything. Our culture seems interested only in asking whether Lindsay Lohan is on drugs or whether Madonna is adopting another baby. Life's deeper questions seem to elude us.

We've become an intellectually lazy society. Skimming headlines, flipping through news channels, and distractedly surfing the Web have left us poorly suited to ask penetrating questions about our existence. Our attention spans are so short we can barely absorb a few paragraphs, let alone an entire book. Heck, we can't even watch TV anymore, preferring instead to channel surf.

We call ourselves one of the most educated nations on earth, because more than 60 percent of the population holds some kind of a college degree. Yet our ignorance is profound. Half of all Americans can't find Iraq on a map. Fewer than 28 percent can name the chief justice of the Supreme Court, and one in five believes that the sun revolves around the earth. More than half of Americans can name at least two characters from *The Simpsons*, while fewer than half that number can name two or more freedoms guaranteed by the First Amendment. While almost three-quarters of Americans recall that Freedom of Speech is one of the Bill of Rights' fundamental guarantees, fewer than a fourth remember that Freedom of Religion is included as well. A full 26 percent of Americans aren't even aware that the United States declared independence from the United Kingdom. We're not ignorant only about history, either. Religion is also increasingly a mystery to us: only half of American adults can name one of the four Gospels, a majority don't know that Genesis is the first book of the Bible, and 10 percent believe that Joan of Arc was Noah's wife!

Nor is it only adults who are hazy on the facts—our children are even worse off. Fewer than half of American teenagers know when the Civil War happened, a quarter think that Columbus sailed to the New World in the 1700s, rather than in 1492, and 25 percent of teenagers aren't sure who Adolf Hitler was. More than half of teenagers don't know that Sudan is a country in Africa, half can't find New York State on a map, and almost that many believe that the majority religion in India is Islam. In one recent study that asked American teenagers to name the world's major religions, not quite half were able to come up with Buddhism, and fewer than half remembered Judaism.

How can we have learned so much, yet know so little? Simple. We studied not because we were curious but because we were greedy. We got degrees to land good jobs, rather than to become enlightened. And what does it say that so many of our universities are party colleges where students get catatonically drunk on a regular basis?

Kids begin life inquisitive about their world. Yet once they start attending school, we swiftly train them to focus on pleasing their teachers and getting good grades to get into college. Once that's done, and they get the jobs they've been coveting, they'll work hard until they can one day retire.

We've turned education into a goal to be completed. Once you've attained it, you put away the books and you pick up *People* and *Us Weekly*. In reality, enlightenment should be a lifelong journey. It never culminates, and it is as limitless as space.

If we can only galvanize our curiosity, our lives will flourish along with our relationships. We will attain higher understanding and deeper perception.

Ask yourself,

Do I really know what's going on in the world? Am I up-to-date with current events? I don't care if I know the names of all of the world leaders or if I'm familiar with the price of gold and oil. That's ephemeral trivia compared to the really important trends in our world. Do I really know whether democracy is growing worldwide? Are human rights advancing, or is someone, somewhere, trampling them? I hear plenty of politicians chattering about America's addiction to oil—but are new sources of energy being developed? Is anyone out there solving these problems or even asking these questions?

My mind defines my individuality. It makes me who I am. If it softens, if I allow it to atrophy, then I shrivel along with it. I'm not going to let that happen. My mind is a muscle, and like any muscle that is not used, it can grow flabby and soft. Later, when I want to do intellectual heavy lifting, I cannot. I am ill-equipped to go deeper in areas where I must.

I look to the travel writer Bill Bryson as a sterling example of a person who always asks. Bryson is a hilarious writer, but what makes his books so compelling is that he sees things about human nature that others miss. What would bore other people in everyday interactions fascinates him, and he captures the nuances of human motivation in his travel books. It was therefore not all that surprising to me that Bryson suddenly appeared with a book titled *A Short History of Nearly Everything.* In the introduction he wrote, "I was on a long flight across the Pacific, staring idly out the window at the moonlit ocean, when it occurred to me with a certain uncomfortable forcefulness that I didn't know the first thing about the only planet I was ever going to live on. I had no idea, for example, why the oceans were salty but the Great Lakes weren't. Didn't have the faintest idea. . . . I didn't know what a proton was, or a protein, didn't know a quark from a quasar, didn't understand how geologists could look at a layer of rock on a canyon wall and tell you how old it was, didn't know anything really." He was inspired by that impulse to learn all of those things he never knew about the world—and, of course, to write a book about it.

Most of us aren't going to write a book like Bryson's, but we can nonetheless resolve to be curious about things that matter. In so doing, we can repair our relationships, refashioning ourselves as better, more engaged people. On the road to revitalizing our curiosity, the first question is one you need to ask yourself.

Turn off the TV, close your eyes, and engage your deepest innermost essence in self-talk. Start with a simple question and ask yourself,

Why do I feel so bored? I feel lethargic, as though I lack the energy I used to have. What's dragging me down? Deep inside, I can sense that there is an emptiness within me.

I know what it is: *I'm losing my innate curiosity.* The things that used to interest me have lost their appeal. I used to read so many books and devour real newspapers, always hungry for more information about my world. Now I tide myself over by reading glossy magazines and other fluff. If I read a book a year, I'm lucky, and often it is a trashy novel that doesn't make me think. I've become so dependent on TV, it's shutting down my mind.

My spouse and I rarely have conversations other than about practical matters. Everything we talk about is the daily grind, the kids, schools, bills, finances, and where we should go on vacation. I can't remember the last time we had a deep conversation about us, our lives, our dreams, our goals and aspirations.

The same is true of my conversations with my kids. Do I really know them? I don't ask them penetrating questions, only the kinds to which they can give me single, monosyllabic responses. I know the names of their teachers, barely, but I don't know what my kids really think of their education. I know some of my kids' friends, but I have little idea of the nature of their relationships. When I try to engage my kids in those types of conversations, they often shut me out. There is a general culture of ignorance around our home, in which nearly everything we talk about is superficial and on the surface. We are losing the capacity to go deeper.

But it's not too late. I want to change, and I know I can. I want to be someone who inspires other people with my wisdom and curiosity. I want my family to flourish, and I want to know my spouse in the deepest possible way. I want to know my kids and to shape them into inquisitive adults. *A superficial life is not acceptable to me—I refuse to live in the shallows.*

From today forward, I'm going to reorient my life away from finding all of the answers to learning how to ask the right questions.

I resolve to *always ask*.

Likewise, I now understand that I know so little about my spouse, and being aware of his or her favorite movie or ice cream flavor doesn't qualify. When was the last time I probed my spouse's sexual mind, asking about his/her fantasies and erotic interests. These are uncomfortable conversations, but they are absolutely necessary if we are to go beyond being two people in a relationship and truly become one flesh.

American society doesn't make it easy to ask questions. As a rule, we tend to *answer* when we should *ask* and even go so far as to look down on those who express their curiosity. Nowhere is this truer than where politics is concerned.

The public sphere has become so poisonous and polarized that common ground between right and left seems beyond our reach. Disagreement, disunion, and anger so define our culture that conservatives and liberals, Republicans and Democrats seem to have nothing to learn from one another. Instead of debating and coming up with the solutions we sorely need, they demonize one another. Even worse, if elected members of either party attempt to compromise with the enemy, they are seen as sellouts and their conservative or liberal credentials are questioned.

No one asks the crucial question: what is my opponent's real motivation? Do the other guys *really* want to destroy the United States? During the run-up to the Iraq war, half of the country said that George W. Bush and his conservative cronies didn't care about Iraqi lives but that he simply wanted to enrich his friends in the oil business. The other half said that liberals didn't care that this brutal tyrant Saddam Hussein was slaughtering and gassing his own people. A rational conversation became nearly impossible. Since then, it's only gotten worse.

Politicians today pretend to have all of the answers, but we are still waiting for a truly effective leader who knows how to ask the right questions and who inspires his or her followers to ponder the answers. I fear that we'll continue to wait a long time.

So, in the absence of that leader, let us use self-talk to remind ourselves to be curious—even about our ideological opponents. The ancient rabbis expressed it best. "Never be dismissive of anything, and never be disparaging of anybody. Because there is nothing that doesn't have its place, and there is no person who doesn't have his time."

As hard as it is to overcome widespread discontent and debate, it's important to ask one another, especially when it seems as if we have nothing in common, "What is your motivation? What is the purpose of your position?" and most important, *"What can I learn from what you're saying?"*

Shove aside the voices of rage, of self-certainty, and engage with the voice of your inner spirit. Say to yourself,

I spend most of my day so certain that I'm right and everyone else is wrong. When I flip on the news and hear a dissenting opinion, I change the channel. I buy books that validate my worldview, rather than challenge it. I listen to those who inflame me against the other side, rather than make me think and be challenged. If my neighbor from across the street reveals that he voted for the other party, I feel disappointed, sensing immediately that something critical divides us. Yet as comfortable as it is for me to live in this cocoon of certainty, I know it's time to challenge myself.

I never want to be afraid to ask.

Starting today, I'm setting aside my pride. As sure as I am of myself, I want to be open to other opinions and not afraid to ask questions about what others think. I'll have an honest discussion with my neighbor about an issue we disagree on. And when we come to an impasse, I won't just become silent and write the person off. This time I'll ask questions. "Why exactly do you feel that way? How did you come to that opinion?"

By and by, we'll find common ground. If he raises a good point or tells me about a historical fact I wasn't aware of, I'll listen, taking his ideas seriously—maybe I'll even get a book out of the library to learn more about the topic at hand.

No longer will I be reluctant to admit what I simply don't know, even though it goes against the grain of American culture—after all, I'm supposed to have all of the answers or at least act as if I do. Maybe brazen people will condemn me for admitting I'm curious and for being willing to listen and ask questions. But thoughtful people will respect me for my honesty, and those are the people I want in my intellectual company.

Maintaining open-mindedness and curiosity is not only a political matter. It's equally important in setting a good example for our children. Erich Fromm pointed out that in today's world, even children pretend to know the answers to everything. I've seen the truth of this firsthand. When I speak at schools, I make sure to quiz the kids on history, geography, and current events. Every time I ask a question, nearly every hand goes up. The students don't necessarily know the answers, but their hands are up anyway. *They are trained to act as if they know, rather than to ask.*

Why is this the case? Because our culture is ignorant of its own ignorance. Even if you don't know, you pretend to know. Spin has replaced substance. BS-ing your way through a subject you're scantly aware of is easier than admitting that you don't know and asking.

To take just one example, we've all seen parents who treat their daughters differently from their sons. I'm not talking only about giving Barbies to girls and baseball gloves to boys. There are age-old gender prejudices that emerge in parents' behavior. A few seconds after giving their girls the sugar-and-spice treatment, mothers and fathers will turn around and act as if they're trying to toughen up their male children. We like to think that we're more enlightened than this, but if we don't pay attention, it can happen. I know I've made this mistake, even though I promised myself I wouldn't.

Don't get me wrong; I have always tried to defy this trend and treat my three sons no differently than my six daughters. If there's a baseball game that I want to watch with my sons, I'll see that my daughters come, too. In many Jewish homes the boys go to synagogue more often than the girls do, but not in our household. If the boys are going somewhere, the girls are coming as well.

In my head, I was being a perfectly fair father at all times. But one day my wife pulled me aside. "Shmuley," she said, "have you noticed how critical you've been of our son lately?"

As I thought about it, it dawned on me that this was completely true. If I gave my daughters one or two criticisms per day, I'd give him five—just like the parents I was trying *not* to imitate, I acted as though I were trying to toughen him up. I realized that if I didn't slow down and quit being so hard on him, it would only be a matter of time until he started to feel as if I were picking on him.

I had to stop short and ask myself,

Why am I doing this? What unconscious urge is pushing me to be a critical father?

If I'm truthful with myself, I know that I'm just doing what my father did to me and what his father did to him, and so on. In the old days, fathers tried to toughen up their sons, to prepare them to be men in a difficult world. I thought I'd moved beyond that, but no matter how enlightened I think I am, there are little tics and impulses lingering under the surface. If I don't take stock of my behavior and ask questions of myself, I could unwittingly cause lifelong animosity and unhappiness.

No, I'm going to start giving my son the compliments he deserves and quit being so critical. And I will continue to be inquisitive about my own behavior as a man and as a father— it's my duty to my children and to myself.

As parents, we have the responsibility to always ask.

So many of us—me included—believe we know our children. Because we have figured them out, we feel as if we have the right, indeed the obligation, to tell them exactly what do to with their lives. This is why you see so many parents helicoptering their children, making every decision for them and refusing to let them do anything independently. No wonder our kids feel so much more comfortable talking to their friends—the ones who make a real effort to find out who they are—than to us.

Not long ago, I sat my older kids down and offered an apology. This is what I said: "When I got married, I promised myself that I would be the greatest father ever. I wanted to give you guys what I didn't have: a wholesome, rather than broken, childhood. I vowed I would be there for you, guide you, and love you. And I did just that. I was always there for you. I raised you, and I smothered you with affection.

"Now, all of these years later—and Mushki, you're already twenty—I realize I *over*did it. I proceeded on the assumption that

I knew everything. Your different characters, your individual passions. Thinking that I had all of the answers, I told each of you what you should be doing and how best to develop your potential.

"I now realize that I made a mistake. I saw you as blocks of limitless potential for me to sculpt into special kids. I *was* supposed to provide the overall framework of values, love, inspiration and guidance. But once I did that, I had to give you the space to be you.

"I confess: I *don't* fully know you. You're my kids, and I love you infinitely. But I am not you. My job now is to provide the latitude to allow the gradual unfolding of your own individual desires and talents. So I'm sorry for being so certain that I never stopped to ask questions."

I meant every word. As a father, I thought I had done everything right. I had given my children all of the answers when the real job of a parent is to be the one who inspires his offspring to ask the right questions. "*Who am I? What is my purpose? What are my unique gifts? And how can I best contribute to my surroundings and make my life purposeful?*" Yet although the parent can inspire those questions, only the child can provide the answers—answers, I might add, that will never be final, because life is an endless journey.

Whether your children are infants or teenagers, it's not too late to instill in them a healthy curiosity about life's mysteries. So engage in self-talk and say,

> In my relationship with my kids, I'm no longer going to make the mistake of thinking I know everything about them. Rather, I'll learn to ask. I'll develop a genuine curiosity about my children's lives, from the practical matters to the much deeper character questions. I'll show them that I have a deep desire to know and understand them. I'll ask them about their favorite teachers, who their close friends are, which subjects they like at school, and what their favorite restaurant is. Then I'm going to dig deeper. I'll ask them what they find fulfilling about their lives and what areas they find uninspiring. Which aspects of their upbringing engage them and which leave them cold. I'll even

ask them what aspects of our relationship they consider solid and which need work. And what mistakes, in their opinion, I make as a parent.

I know I need to avoid the pat questions that make my children feel as if I'm simply trying to manipulate or motivate them. I'm not going to bother asking them what they want to do when they get older. That's for them to determine. Instead, I'll ask them what or who they want to be, what kind of qualities they want to develop, and what kind of virtue they would like to foster in themselves.

My kids often complain that I don't listen. They don't mean that I'm distracted on a phone call or watching TV, which is often true enough. They mean that as a parent, I'm a know-it-all. And it's humbling to discover just how much I don't know.

I resolve to make the "always ask" philosophy central to my parenting.

Many of the people I speak to these days are on some kind of spiritual quest. Fed up with the suffocating materialism that surrounds us, they have embarked on a search for something higher. More often than not, however, religion fails them. The reason: most religions teach us not to ask questions but rather to consider those questions settled, thanks to their often pat answers.

The problem with this approach is that it makes faith into a destination, rather than a journey, a place to be reached, instead of a road to be traveled. It can quickly become boring. People go to places of worship and often find the environment stifling.

Don't get me wrong. I'm a passionately religious Jew. I love and live religion, and I respect my brothers and sisters of all faiths. Religious ritual is incredibly important to me. But faith is supposed to inspire you to ask the great questions of life, so that you become a deeper, more spiritual person, rather than a know-it-all with a shallow sense of moral purpose.

Here is an example. The greatest question in religion is, Why does God allow evil to flourish? Where is God when the righteous suffer? I have been obsessed with this question all of my life and have devoted an entire book to it, *Wrestling with the Divine: A Jewish Response to Suffering.* Now, religions offer three standard answers to the question of why a good God allows innocent people to suffer. The first is sin. People deserve their suffering. It is, of course, a grossly inadequate explanation. Really, a million children who were gassed in the Holocaust committed some terrible sin?

Then there is the second response: we mortals don't know the mind of God. Our brains are too puny to understand God's cosmic reasons. What may appear to us to be senseless suffering really has a higher purpose. In what universe, however, could what the Tutsis experienced, being macheted to death at the rate of three hundred an hour for three months by the Hutus in Rwanda in 1994, constitute anything other than savage suffering? Could it really be that from God's perspective, this was something good? As a child withers away from leukemia, are we really going to say that God has some higher purpose, that the parent's unimaginable suffering is somehow a blessing? I know a woman whose son died of cancer at age ten. The woman goes to the cemetery every single day and cries for hours. It's been going on for years, and no one can comfort her. Will any cleric approach this woman and tell her that what happened is somehow redemptive?

Finally, there is the third answer: suffering is ennobling. It refines our character. It makes us into better people. It teaches us what's really important in life. Only through death do we discover the infinite value of life. This is the response that bothers me the most. I have counseled thousands of people. The ones who suffered the most are scarred the most. Yes, they may have gained some enlightenment through all of their suffering, but it is so often drowned in an ocean of pessimism and gloom. Suffering leaves us not wiser but more cynical, not more committed but more broken, not elevated but depressed.

The true response is to ask a question. "God Almighty, You have taught us that life is precious and that the good are rewarded with happy lives. So, why does this not work in practice? We will continue to ask the question, not until You give us an answer but until You remove suffering from the earth. And until You do so, we will do our best, limited as we are as mortal human beings, to cure disease, fight hunger, and abolish war. Because we don't want to *understand* suffering but to eradicate it."

Most Americans would prefer to have black-and-white answers. They want to know that God has blond hair or a long white beard. They would prefer a miniaturized idol that they can slip into their pocket. This impulse is why Sigmund Freud said that religion was a neurosis, Karl Marx called it an opiate, and Christopher Hitchens said it was a poison (among many other things). All of these men were responding to the idea that religion is crafted for the superstitious person who craves certainty.

I've always told my children that there is another kind of religious person—someone in whom religion incites questions. "Why am I here? Who is God? What am I supposed to do with my life? How can we make the world more perfect?" I believe that the truly religious person does not seek answers and certainty—the truly religious man is so courageous that he is willing to devote his life to permanently searching and asking questions.

Where religion is concerned, you have to encourage questioning—both in yourself and in your children. I can't stress this enough: *we can't be afraid of our children's questions.* If we worry that they will expose our own ignorance, we'll end up giving them silly answers and punishing them for their curiosity.

Our children sometimes have the power to ask us the most difficult questions of all. I brought my eldest daughter with me to Haiti, three weeks after the devastating earthquake. We passed through a morgue filled with three hundred people—horrible but, as we learned, these were the lucky ones, because at least their bodies were kept safe. We soon saw a nursing college where nurses' bodies were being eaten by scavenging dogs. The corpses of children and babies were strewn everywhere. The stench of death and decay was so bad that we couldn't keep from gagging. Horrors surrounded us, and there were sights in Haiti that haunt us still.

As we walked through this horrific tableau, my daughter turned to me and said, "This is shaking my faith in God's goodness; how could God have let this happen to all of these innocent people?"

She was having a very real crisis—and what was I supposed to say in response? I could have told her that it wasn't God but rather the devil who was at fault, as some Christians believe. Alternately, I could have used the argument of some orthodox Jews, who claim that only by having both sides, good and evil, could we choose to believe in God. I might also have picked the Deist strategy and said that God created the world and then left it to its own devices. But I dismissed all of these easy answers.

My response was, "That's a very good question. *God has a lot of explaining to do.* When you witness this kind of devastation, you have every right to challenge God and demand to know how He could allow it." Did God really need my defense at that moment? Instead, I chose not to brush off my daughter's curiosity but to stoke it.

We tend to give pat answers to our children because we're afraid of challenging our own faith. What we need to accept is that relations with God are dynamic, filled with push and pull, moments of comfort and agitation, moments of certainty followed by doubt. In this way, faith is like a candle that flickers. Yet because we ask questions, it never goes out.

Religion is supposed to awaken you to the infinite aspect of existence and the limitless nature of life. More than anything else, it's supposed to inspire you to *ask*—rather than answer—questions.

In fact, this is precisely why Judaism is such an unsatisfying religion to so many people. Every other religion attempts to tell you exactly where you're going to go when you die, what God looks like, what happens in Hell, in Heaven, and so on. Judaism makes no attempt to answer these questions. We can speculate. We can argue.

We can debate. Yet ultimately, we recognize that a courageous journey into the unknown is the mark of a true believer.

*To cease to question is to allow our intellect to
die and to let our faith become worthless.*

Be brave in your questioning of yourself and your God. Gather up your courage and say to yourself,

I want to ask the right questions in my relationship with God.

I categorically reject the idea that in my relationship with God, I can only be submissive. I want no part of any religion that teaches me that I am merely cosmic chaff, that whatever God does is just, and that my role is solely to bow my head in silent submission, accepting that my puny human brain can never understand the ways of the Lord. That silly idea promotes not only complacency but fraudulence in my relationship with God.

I never want to be afraid to ask God the most challenging questions of existence: "God, why do the righteous suffer? Why is there so much evil in the world? How can You be silent in times like these?"

There is so much I need to ask God—"What is my place in the world, oh Lord, and what do You expect of me? Why do You hide, and when will You ever make Yourself known? What is my destiny, and why did You put me on this earth? How can I find meaning in my life and favor in Your presence, oh Lord?"

I have so many questions to ask God, and I'll never cease asking them. I know, even in the process of questioning, that I draw closer to Him. That's why I must always ask.

Life is a journey of exploration in which curiosity is the most important component. Always asking helps people conquer the shame of not knowing an answer—moreover, it keeps them from assuming that they already know all of life's mysteries. A poignant aphorism in the Talmud says, "The man who is shy will never learn." Most of all, this is true for relationships.

I have counseled so many men and women who have lost their curiosity about each other. They've allowed preconceived notions about their partners to crystallize into certainties. After years of cohabitation, they never ask each other anything. Their sexual connection has been nearly extinguished, and they can barely remember their last serious conversation.

When I meet these people, I am always reminded of an old story. There was a great rabbi who had only one daughter—a very scholarly and kind woman. The rabbi wanted to find a special man for his daughter to wed, so he traveled to a famous rabbinical college and announced that any student who could answer a very difficult question on the Talmud would gain his daughter's hand in marriage.

The next day, hundreds of yeshiva students lined up to attempt to answer the question. Yet no one could get it right.

The next day only fifty lined up. Then thirty-five. Then ten. Then no one.

Finally, the rabbi got up, sadly thanked the students for trying, hitched his horse to the buggy, and started to ride away.

Yet behind him, in the distance, he saw a young man chasing after him with a huge volume of the Talmud. The rabbi stopped his buggy because he assumed that the boy wanted to attempt to answer the question. But to his surprise, the boy told him that he didn't have an answer. He simply wanted to know what the answer was.

The great rabbi got off the horse, grabbed the student by his coat, and said to him, "You're the one." Baffled, the student argued with the rabbi that he didn't *know* the answer. He just wanted to learn what it was. And the rabbi said to him, "You're the one. You're the groom I was searching for. That's all I wanted. I wasn't looking for a know-it-all or an arrogant show-off. *I was looking for someone who is genuinely curious.*

"I want someone who wants to know my daughter, who wants to explore life with her and believes that they have so much to learn together. Yes, you are the one!"

This story holds an important lesson for all of us who think our marriage is unsalvageable—and it is particularly relevant for our own incurious society. American culture trains us to fill the emptiness of our existence with things, instead of asking how we can repair our relationships. We are subtly conditioned to fill our lives with electronic gadgets, closets full of clothes. Everything is treated as a commodity to be bought, an object to be owned. That kind of lifestyle isn't working.

We need to make the "Always ask" philosophy a fundamental part of how we relate to one another.

So, husbands, speak to the voice of your innermost self, and admit the truth:

My wife complains that I don't listen—and I know that she's often right. The truth is, we just don't talk enough. And when we do, it's either about the most practical aspects of our lives or simply to argue.

I'm also beginning to understand that I lecture my wife. I sometimes speak to her as if she's one of the kids. I tell her how we ought to run the house, raise the kids, and spend our money. I don't listen enough, and I certainly don't ever ask her about anything.

So I'm committing to change, and my first step will be to ask questions.

First, I'll ask her how her day was. How was work? What did she do with the kids? Is she tired? Is there something I can do to help?

Next, I'll inquire about her emotional life. How is she feeling? How are her spirits? How am I as a husband? Is there something I can do to be a better man and to make her happier? These aren't easy questions to ask. I admit that I'm afraid of some of the answers. No husband wants to hear that he isn't doing a good enough job. No one wants to feel inadequate. But I won't be afraid to ask. I would rather hear something hurtful that I can put right than allow my wife to nurse a legitimate grievance that I can correct.

This especially applies to my actions as a lover. I love my wife, but our marriage is growing stale. Our sex life has become a rut of predictable sex, once a week, for maybe ten minutes at best. My wife deserves better than these passionless quickies. My first responsibility as a husband is to make her feel like a woman. My wife gives me her all. She deserves to feel desirable. And it's my responsibility to revitalize my desire.

I have to admit that part of the reason I am losing some of my attraction to her is that I think I know her inside and out. I treat her like a book I've already read.

But no more. I'm going to keep asking questions—even the toughest questions of all. I will boldly ask the erotic questions that will allow me to truly know her as a wife. We men make the mistake of believing that our wives are not as sexual as we are, that they are not as attracted to the opposite sex as we are. But we're wrong.

I'm going to sit with my wife on a regular basis and come to know her as a woman in full. "Do I satisfy you as a lover? Do I, as a man, always make you feel desirable? Are all of your sexual needs being fulfilled in this marriage?"

Then, even more painful questions. "Are there men besides me to whom you are attracted? Do any of them reciprocate your attraction? Are there men in general who you think are interested in you? Do you ever think about them? Do you think about them in sexual situations?" The answers may hurt my pride, but there is no true erotic lust without a measure of frustrated desire and pain. Besides, it is only when a husband understands his wife's insatiable sexual needs that he begins to pursue her all over again.

I'm going to ask my wife about her sexual fantasies. She may at first be embarrassed to reveal them, but I'll tease them out. I want to know the inner recesses of her erotic mind. I don't want any part of her closed off to me.

That's exactly what I'll do: I'm going to save our marriage, and my method will be to *always ask*.

As we know from experience, nothing in marriage is one-size-fits-all—so in this case the self-talk runs a bit differently for wives. I say to my female readers, "Speak for yourselves, completely independently from your husband's voice. Push away the inner voices of hurt feelings and frustration, of defensiveness and of coldness. Find the voice of authenticity within yourself and admit the truth."

I know that my husband doesn't always feel appreciated. He comes home and he's quiet. He feels that he works hard for the family but that we don't always show complete appreciation. He retreats into himself. He sulks or he watches TV.

It's not as if I haven't tried to perk him up. I try to ask him questions, but I now realize that I haven't been asking the right ones. I've been asking him practical, yes-or-no questions, and I get monosyllabic responses in return. I can do better. I want to be the person to whom he unburdens himself emotionally, the one to whom he opens up.

I will start asking him questions about his feelings. I'll make myself the outlet for his heart. Instead of asking, "How was your day at work?" and getting a grunt in return, I'll ask him, "How do you feel about your job?" "What's your feeling about how your boss treats you?" "Do you feel that this job you're doing is what you want to do? Do you feel as if they appreciate you at work? How does the job you're doing match your original professional expectations?" As he expands beyond monosyllables, we'll suddenly find that we're communicating as never before.

I'll also try to address his ego issues. Does he feel good about himself as a man? How is he coping with our financial pressures? Does the fact that we have challenges paying our bills leave him feeling bad about himself?

I want him to know that I am here for him, in sickness and in health, and I adore him for the work that he does and the man that he is.

Most important, I want our marriage to be passionate. I don't want a mere *partner* in my life. The very term is cold and distant. It's not as if I'm opening a business with my husband. We are not collaborators in the exercise of running a home, nor are we coworkers in the job of raising our children.

What I want is a soul mate. I need someone with whom I bond intimately and spiritually. Someone with whom I become bone of one bone and flesh of one flesh. To achieve that end, I need to ask the right questions. Starting today, I vow to do exactly that.

In our world we are trained to devour, to imbibe, to own, and to acquire. When we start life, we are largely empty vessels. If the question is, "What will we fill our lives with?" society will tell us to fill it with objects, money, and other people's approval. We all know where those things will lead us. Listen instead to curiosity's response, which is, "Fill yourself with knowledge." Plug the hole with information.

In everything you do, always ask. If you're sitting in class, listen attentively to the teacher. Don't tune out. If you're in a new job, find out what leads to true success. Apprentice yourself to someone who is a master. If you're in a relationship, don't be content with a superficial connection. Ask questions. Seek intimacy. Peel away the layers of the person you love and delve into his or her infinite essence.

Heed the call. Be inquisitive, and your life and relationships will be inexhaustible. Just always, always ask.

To develop a personalized relationship with the voice of your innermost self, ask yourself the following questions. Respond to them, and let the answers guide you on self-talks of your own devising.

Am I a motivated person?

If I am a student, am I ashamed to ask questions in class?

When people tell me something new, do I always jump in and say, "Oh, yes, I knew that" or, "Yep, heard about that," and close myself off to further discussion? Or am I receptive to new information?

Do I allow myself to be challenged by people around me, or do I confine myself to talking only to those who tell me what I want to hear?

Do I show people I'm a hothead so that whenever something serious is on the line, people don't want to tell me about it, because they know I can't handle my emotions?

If there is trouble in my life, do I seek counseling? Am I afraid to admit my problems? Have I truly engaged with my innermost self, the essence of my identity, to bridge the gap between how I currently behave and the kind of person I aspire to be?

10

Know Your Gift

CONVERSATION 10

I will rise above comparing myself to others and focus on my unique contribution.

Now for the finale: the tenth and final conversation you need to have with yourself. As I'm sure you can imagine, we've saved the best for last.

A few months ago, I asked twenty guests at my Friday night Sabbath dinner to raise their hands if they had found their place in the world. Most were respected professionals working in television, publishing, banking, and politics, yet only two hands went up. Times may be hard, but for me, this was eye-opening. Are so many people really that unhappy with themselves?

The malaise I witnessed in my guests is all too common. It isn't isolated to any group or cross section of society; the whole of the country feels it, and no politician can rescue us. Between sky-high unemployment and an electorate that swerves from party to party, no one feels good about where we're headed. We thought Obama was the messiah but then quickly grew tired of the redeemer. No doubt, some other great savior will arise, and we'll become disillusioned with him or her as well.

Previous crises always had an identifiable external cause that could be remedied, however painfully. During the Civil War, it was slavery; during the Great Depression, it was high tariffs. In World War II, it was Hitler. These days, there is no external cause. The enemy is us. Americans are unhappy because they are trapped in lives not their own.

Between the money we're supposed to be making, the fashions we have to wear, and the TV shows we're told to watch, most choices in our culture have become standardized. Sure, there are still a few important ones, but they nearly all fit into some existing structure. Whether you're choosing between the political right and left, picking among the eight Ivy League colleges, or choosing a career, your life is designed to fit into external expectations.

No wonder we feel ordinary. We're haunted by the niggling feeling that we don't fit in and, even worse, that our achievements are doomed to be inadequate. As our metabolism slows down and new gray hairs sprout, every day makes us unhappier about who we've become.

What we seem to have forgotten is that God does not send us into the world empty-handed.

Every person is born with an inner package—a gift that we were meant to contribute to the world. Failing to act on that gift deprives the universe of a crucial element, throwing all things out of balance. That's why the Ten Commandments forbid murder: by removing someone from this world, you unilaterally snuff out his or her contribution, disturbing the perfectly honed equilibrium of the universe. Your gift sets you apart from everyone else and makes your life essential. Only the voice of your innermost self can reveal to you what your gift is.

Over the years, I've met countless people who needed help finding that gift. Charles was an IT professional who came to me for counseling. He was well liked at work and made good money, but he still wasn't happy. His wife, Julie, recognized the signs: he was withdrawn, detached, and, in a word, depressed. When they came to see me, I asked Charles why he was so unhappy.

He shrugged his shoulders. "Look at me. I fix computers for a living. It's not that it isn't meaningful, it just feels insignificant. I keep remembering that when I was in college, I always thought I would do something bigger than this. I thought I was going to make a difference in life, and I'm disappointed."

"Charles," I said. "Don't you realize that even the world's most accomplished people sometimes look back at their lives and ask what they could have done differently? That impulse is completely natural. It's hardwired into all of us because God doesn't want us to squander our potential. He therefore gave each of us a seeker's impulse. Besides, even if you were to win elected office or become a major philanthropist, your life wouldn't suddenly become meaningful. Defining yourself by other people's standards won't help you contribute your gift to the world. Your gift is yours alone.

"Instead of kicking yourself for not living up to others' expectations, you need to establish what your gift actually is. Tell me, what are you good at?"

He sat back and thought for a moment. Then he said, "You know, it's amazing how frustrated people get when their technology quits. Their BlackBerry goes dead, or they lose a file they've worked on, and they come to me enraged. Everyone tells me that I'm good at calming people down, helping them find perspective. And if it turns out we can't recover their documents, I remind them that sometimes it's a secret blessing. If you retype your report while it's fresh in your mind, more often than not it's even better than the original. People end up walking away a little less furious."

I nodded and said, "Now *that's* amazing. You have the ability to make everyone around you see the positive in the world. Everyone, that is, except you. What an amazing gift! Now don't you think it's time for you to share it with yourself?"

Charles had thought that all he did in life was fix computers, but in truth his gift was something far more rare. He had a talent for fixing people. He was a healer, even though he couldn't see it at first. By learning to recognize his gift, he was able to find new value in his job, his family, and himself.

Just as it did for Charles, seeking out your gift can be extraordinarily good for your mental outlook. If you've read this far, you have the tools to find it within yourself. All of the conversations in chapters before this one can contribute to locating your gift. Only by becoming self-aware, recognizing your motivations for what they are, and attuning yourself to the voices within can you identify what makes you truly unique.

Sit down, reactivate that voice of your inner self, and ask,

How do I feel about myself? If I'm completely honest, I feel as if I'm bursting at the seams!

Waking up is the hardest part of my day, because that's the moment I realize that I need to go through the same rigmarole once again. I have to go through the motions, all day long, and so much of it bores me. I *know* that I have so much to offer, but I don't know whom I should give it to or how.

What I need to do, what I know I *have* to do, is find *my* place in the world. I have to stop living on autopilot. I need to take a step back and decide whether the life I'm living is my own or someone else's.

I have to know my gift, and I'm ready to do the work to find out what it is.

I'll admit that on first blush, knowing your gift may not *sound* all that difficult.

You may say to yourself, "My gift is being a good cook. My spouse, on the other hand, is an expert carpenter. End of story." Knowing your gift is a bit more complicated, however. We often equate gifts with "talents," calling a great pianist or our bright child gifted. Your true gift is something much more complex.

Other readers may protest, "What's so hard about knowing my gift? Mine's easy—it's that I'm a hard worker with an impressive net worth." But that's not your life's gift at all, although I can't blame you for thinking so. Our culture leads us to define ourselves by comparison with others. *Who is the biggest earner? Who has the most expensive house? Who's going to the best and most exclusive restaurant?* Yet none of these questions has anything to do with who we really are. Your true gift is something altogether unique.

The greatest mistake you can make is to live according to the standards of others. Seeking to be the next Warren Buffett or Brad Pitt will never fulfill you—there will always be someone richer or more famous. After all, in America *everyone* wants to be wealthy and renowned. Yet although we can compete endlessly against one another for external advantages, competition itself becomes irrelevant with regard to our innate gift.

Rather than a talent or a bank account, your gift is your unique contribution to the world. It sums up all of the goodness that you have to offer. It defies comparison. No one else's gift is exactly like yours. If you maintain an awareness of what makes you different from everyone else, you will never lack purpose or value in life.

For those of you who don't know what your gift is, I've boiled my method down to five questions. Seek out your voice of authenticity, deep inside, and ask the following, then take note of what you come up with.

1. What experiences have most scarred you in your life, and from what do you most need to heal?

What most scars you is whatever touches you the deepest, the event that casts the longest shadow over your life. This experience also has the strange tendency of remaining in the picture long after you heal from it, focusing you like a laser beam on how you can bring healing to others. In my case, because my parents divorced when I was a boy, I have focused on healing hearts and families.

My career has been devoted to overcoming my own formative scarring event. Few things give me as much satisfaction as saving a doomed marriage.

The scars that we experience sensitize us to the scarring of others. Christopher Hitchens and I have publicly debated religion and the existence of God four separate times over the years. Each successive debate was harsher and less gracious. After he wrote the book *God Is Not Great: How Religion Poisons Everything*, he became, in my opinion, radicalized, seeming to dislike not only religion but perhaps religious people themselves.

Yet things changed after he was diagnosed with esophageal cancer. As soon as I found out, I wrote a column titled "My Prayer for a Worthy Opponent," wishing him a speedy recovery and detailing how I had asked my thousands of Facebook friends all over the world to pray for his recovery. I sent him a case of wine with the message, "This is a toast to your health. L'chaim!" Soon afterward, when I spoke to him on my radio show, he informed me that the most surprising thing for him was how his former religious opponents were praying for and not against him. He hadn't budged an inch about the existence of God and still thought religion was poison. Fair enough. Yet he was starting to change his mind about the value of religious *people*. Indeed, our last debate together on the question of the afterlife in New York City was far more amicable, even though it was just as substantive.

The painful experience of Hitchens's cancer diagnosis may turn him from a take-no-prisoners enemy of religion into a more measured critic—something religion could use more of. If this turns out to be Hitchens's gift to the world, aside from his many brilliant and erudite columns, it will be all the more true, as I have elsewhere written, that God has reserved a special place for Christopher Hitchens.

The best way to confront your own scarring experience is through self-talk. Ask yourself,

What is the defining event of my life? It could have happened when I was a young child, or it may be more recent. Either way, it's the foundational trauma that I've yet to recover from, and that haunts me still.

What was it? Did my parents ignore me in a time of need? Has addiction, abuse, or poverty touched my life? What is the tender spot in my life's history? I need to know the answer, because it is almost surely the key to finding my gift. If I can find it, it will bring me that much closer to making my mark on the world.

This leads us to the second question, vaulting from trauma to its opposite: your life's inspiration.

2. What experiences have most inspired you in your life and what most lifts you up?

More often than not, the thing that most inspires you will turn out to be the direct inverse of that which has scarred you. Just as my formative wound was enmity and divorce, what has most inspired me is seeing love and joy. During my teen years, until I got married at twenty-one, I used to look at couples on airplanes who traveled together. I loved seeing them. They were never alone. Their home traveled with them. When I got married, it was important to me that if I went somewhere, my wife would come with me. Now, with nine kids, as challenging as it may sound, I try to take our children with us everywhere as well.

Nothing makes me feel more purposeful than bringing people together. At our Friday night Sabbath table, we host Jews and non-Jews, whites and blacks, Christians and Muslims, atheists and agnostics, straight people and gay people, Americans and non-Americans, men and women. Finding the common bond that unites us lifts me up every time, especially when it's in celebration of the beauty and serenity of God's Sabbath.

The same is true for others. I know a woman who lost her young daughter to cancer. She now spends her time appreciating life and volunteering at hospitals. Her gift and inspiration is to give hope to people who have lost theirs.

Ask yourself,

What has most brightened my life? It surely isn't surfing the Web, which is how I spend a large part of my day. Yet although my life can seem bleak and boring when viewed from a certain angle, it also has so many blessings, so many moments that lift me up.

Making other people happy inspires me—but how? It seems that ever since I experienced the trauma of alcoholism, my inspiration has been helping others live cleaner, healthier lives. Or, it may be that since I went through a difficult childhood, losing one of my parents, I have been most inspired by helping troubled children—including and especially my own—find stability in life. And through it all, what inspires me always seems to be connected to my life's own unique travails.

The next question will bring you even closer to finding your gift by drawing from both your scars and your inspirations to find out where they intersect.

3. What activity do you undertake that makes you feel most purposeful?

Odds are, you'll feel most purposeful and best identify your gift when doing something that both heals you from your scarring and reflects what most inspires you.

I know a man named Daniel who grew up in abject poverty and built his own shoe business from scratch. Daniel's greatest scar was a childhood memory of seeing his single mother cry when she was fired from her job and thus could not feed her family. Perhaps for that reason, Daniel's greatest inspiration is to see people's faces light up after a financial miracle. What most gives him purpose are the seminars he conducts and pays for, teaching people who have lost their jobs how to write proper résumés and successfully take part in job interviews. His life has sculpted his character so that he, and only he, is perfectly equipped to contribute this unique gift to the world. This is also why it satisfies him more than it would any other person.

Sort through the memories you have already unearthed, then pinpoint what gives you purpose in life. Say to yourself,

Amid the day-to-day grind, there have been real moments of value and goodness in my life. These intermittent instances of feeling useful are exactly what I'm looking for.

What were they? How did they come about? There was the time I volunteered to help a neighbor repair a fence after a storm. Or how about when I donated some money to disaster relief after watching the news? There was the time I helped a friend get over a difficult breakup and also when I counseled a relative about a death in the family. What do all of these things have in common? Is it my gift to volunteer to help others? If I can only get to the bottom of what gives me a feeling of purpose, I'll be well on my way to finding out.

It needs to be said: these first three questions aren't so simple for everyone. Sometimes preconceptions about yourself can obscure your view. That's why you need to ask the next question, turning to the people who know you best.

4. What do your truest friends most value about you?

Few people know you as your friends do. They see both the good and the bad, yet despite your worst characteristics, they choose to remain friends with you. The most amazing thing about friendship is that it is voluntary. If you had no good qualities for people to like, they probably wouldn't bother trying.

Think about what your friends discuss with you and the advice they seek. Maybe you have a special talent for helping people with low self-esteem. You might be able to divine people's motivation. Your girlfriends might ask you what their boyfriends' intentions are about specific things. Your golfing buddies might inquire about how they should speak to their children because you have a way with words. These are among the best clues you have for discovering your true gift.

Strike up a conversation with your closest friend, and ask him or her, "What do you really like about me? What makes you want to stay my friend?" Your friend may give a superficial answer at first, saying that he or she likes you because you're fun or you have a good sense of humor. But if you engage with your friends deeply, you'll find that they are far more objective about your qualities, good and bad, than you could ever be.

This leads us to the final question, the culmination of the previous four, and perhaps the most difficult question you'll ever have to ask yourself.

5. If you could write your own obituary and choose what you most wish to be remembered for, what would it be?

Sounds morbid, huh? Well, it's not. I'm not here to scare the living daylights out of you by bringing up your own demise. Yet isn't it the darnedest thing? Ninety percent of our personal strivings are not actually what we want to be remembered for. That's because we go through most of our lives in a state of distraction. We don't hear that inner voice I have been trying to bring forth in your mind throughout this book. We do what we want to do, yes—but not what we *really, truly* want.

Think about it. How would your life look after the curtain goes down and the credits start to roll? That's when you'll have the opportunity to ask, Was my life a success? Did I pursue important things or trivial things? Did I matter? And most important, did I contribute my own unique gift?

The best way to answer these questions is to look at them from the objective perspective of an obituary. Trust me, it works.

I once counseled the family of a New York City firefighter named Ron. Although he was a hero to his community, Ron was having serious issues at home. He was isolating himself more and more from his family. Between work and hanging out with his friends, he was out of the house far too frequently and did not spend nearly enough time with his kids. Worse—after a brief separation from his wife, he became jealous, thinking that she had had an affair. Something had to change. But how, I asked myself, could I get him to recommit to his wife and kids?

I asked Ron to put on a suit and a tie and meet me in a local synagogue. He did, with no idea of what he should expect. When he walked in, the synagogue was completely empty except for me, standing at the pulpit, and a long rectangular box covered with a prayer shawl.

From the pulpit I asked him to sit down. Just as it dawned on Ron that the box was a coffin, I began a eulogy. "Dearly beloved," I intoned, "we are gathered here before the earthly remains of Ron to celebrate his life and mourn his passing. He was a good man who led a very interesting life. Every Sunday he would leave his kids at home and go to an auto show. He was a loving husband, at least for the first seven years of his married life, after which he and his wife split because he was convinced, with little to no evidence, that she had betrayed him. He was an amazing friend to his male buddies and went to ball games with them and watched football at home. But he rarely threw a baseball or a football to his own child because there wasn't a lot of time left over in his schedule. At least, he meant well.

"He is mourned by his wife and children, though fortunately they aren't terribly crushed because they long ago had to make peace with his repeated absences. Still, they wish he could have lived so that he could repair the damage he did to the family. He will be sorely missed."

Ron went pale and looked absolutely stunned. He was silent for more than an hour. When I spoke with him afterward, he said he was positively spooked but so overwhelmed that he could not say much more. He had never thought about the serious mistakes he was making in life and how he was squandering his gift.

Don't waste any more time. Cease waiting in the wings for your turn to take control of your life, and begin a self-talk this very moment by asking yourself,

What makes me special? What makes me unique? What distinguishes me from others? If all of the external layers of my being could be stripped away so that only my bare essence remained, what would it be?

I'm starting to realize that it's nothing like the life I'm living. I've fallen into routines and habits that are utterly contrary to my strengths. I'm great at inspiring people to do good, to change their lives and improve themselves—so why do I work in an office all day, doing busywork and punching the clock? I should be living and contributing my gift. What's holding me back?

I think of what Henry David Thoreau wrote in his book *Walden*: "I went to the woods because I wished to live deliberately . . . and not, when I came to die, discover that I had not lived. I wanted to live deep and suck out all the marrow of life . . . to put to rout all that was not life."

Like Thoreau, my fear is that at the end of it all, I will discover that I lived someone else's life. That I never knew my gift and therefore ended up desperately trying to contribute someone else's.

But I'm putting all of those fears to rest. I've looked at my scars, my inspirations, the sources of my sense of purpose, and what my friends see in me. I've looked at my life through the prism of my own obituary, and I see now that although my gift is there, inside me, I have yet to offer it fully to the world.

I will never allow myself to lead a life of regret. The time to change has arrived, and this time I will not let it pass me by.

I vow to contribute my newfound gift, starting now.

So many of us either fail to identify or otherwise forget about our gift. It's important to bear in mind the consequences of squandering our gift. They can be steep, to say the least.

I once counseled Sherri, a headhunter working at an employment agency. Her husband, Carl, was a professor at a university. He'd written a few successful academic books and expected that he would be promoted when his superior retired. When the job was given to someone else, Carl became bitter and morose.

Carl went on an unpaid sabbatical. Sherri supported him but had a hard time respecting him. Her once-impressive academic husband was now aimless, watching TV, speaking only in monosyllables. In an attempt to make a connection with someone she *could* respect, she had an affair with a colleague. When she left her e-mail account open and Carl learned what she was up to, he confronted her.

He said, "Look at me—I've hit rock bottom. I have absolutely nothing to give. Nothing to contribute. So I understand what you're doing. In fact, I not only forgive you, but I think you did the right thing. I have nothing to give to you, and I *am* nothing. If I were you, I would have done the same thing."

I'm sorry to say it, but this story doesn't have a happy ending. Weeks later, Carl took his own life. No one could get through to him. Not even his own wife could lift him up. A man who had once aspired to so much destroyed himself because he felt that he had nothing to give the world.

These are the true stakes of forgetting your gift. Once you start to believe that you're worthless and purposeless, there's no telling what desperate acts you'll commit. Saying that you have no gift is tantamount to saying, "If I exit planet Earth tomorrow, no one would even notice. I contribute nothing, and the world wouldn't miss me if I was gone."

If you ever start to feel as if your time has passed and that you don't have anything to offer, engage yourself in serious self-talk right away. Say to yourself firmly,

God doesn't make mistakes. I know I've been feeling down lately. When I examine my life, I have a hard time seeing what the real value is. But it's there. My existence was called forth by God Almighty. He gave me something that no amount of money can buy. A mind, a heart, eyes, a body, emotions, and thoughts. No laboratory can re-create it, and once it's gone, no one on earth can restore it.

Life *has* to be for a reason. There is no person on earth who doesn't have a gift. If I have begun to feel as if I don't have

anything to contribute, I need to either ask for help in finding it or realize that I may have discarded it, thinking it wasn't
valuable enough.

If I had it once, I can find it again. And I need to remember
that once I identify my gift, even in the most cursory way, I'll
begin to feel such grace. There is no pleasure greater than what
you experience when your gift is given freely. I want, more than
anything, to find my way back to that feeling.

I resolve to remember my own gift and return myself to a
life that contributes.

Once you do find your gift again, your problems won't by any
means have been solved. It's not a panacea. Your gift won't pay your
rent, pick up the kids from school, or get you a better job. It will,
however, mean that the *most important* problem is solved. And that
makes it well worth the effort of seeking it out.

Each of our children is born with an innate gift, just as we were
before them. As parents, we have a special role in helping them cultivate it. It is incumbent on us to assist them, yet it is just as important
that we remember that the gift is theirs alone.

We believe we know what's best for our children. Based on our
own hard-fought experiences, we think we have discovered the key
to succeeding in the world. Maybe so, but it's only *our* personal key
that we've discovered—not theirs.

Our children have so much life, so many experiences ahead of
them—we can't allow our own prejudices to interfere with their
journey.

I've experienced this firsthand. My father grew up impoverished.
When he married my mother and immigrated to the United States,
he intended to make his mark on the world through business so
that he and his family would never again be subjected to the penury
of his youth. Moreover, having risen from insecurity and poverty,

he wanted to raise children who would continue in his footsteps and become successful in their own right.

For this reason, when I told him I wanted to be a rabbi, it disturbed him deeply. I was blessed with countless opportunities he didn't have—college, stability, the American dream—and now I was just throwing it away, cloistering myself in a religious ivory tower. He tried to dissuade me, and it turned into a vociferous debate. I convinced him to let me go to yeshiva on the condition that I would return after one year. But the year that I spent studying holy texts proved to me even more strongly that I was meant to be a rabbi.

I called him up and said, "Abba, I know we made an agreement. But we have to change our agreement. I am not a lawyer, nor am I a businessman. I never will be. I am someone who wants to heal people. That's my gift to the world, and I need to follow it, or else I'll spend the rest of my life regretting it." He was extremely reluctant. To the extent that he consented, it was only because he saw how stubborn I was. Yet in time he came to respect what I do, thank God, and today takes pride in my being a rabbi.

I recently went through the very same argument with my daughter. I thought that I knew what was best for her. I wanted her to go to college here in the United States. But after one year, her heart drew her to Israel. She was charmed by the strength of the people of Israel, carving out a stronghold in the desert, surrounded by enemies but flourishing just the same. She felt an incredible pull to be part of that dream—the youthfulness, dynamism, and bravery of that culture. She wanted to move there and finish her degree in Jerusalem.

I tried to bargain with her. "Okay," I said. "You can move to Israel in just a few years. Israel's the Jewish homeland, the promised land. I love that you want to commit your life to Israel. But get your degree first." Yet I was wrong. Israel was the perfect environment for her to contribute her gift to the world, and she had to go there. She is currently a student at Hebrew University in Jerusalem. I had to remind myself, "I can't create my children in my own image. I have to give them guidance but also let them blossom and come into their gifts on their own."

We parents have to walk a very fine line, supporting our children without predetermining their destiny. My solution is to have open, honest conversations with my kids, enumerating their gifts as I see them and reminding them of their incredible promise.

I gather four of my children together and start a conversation:

"Every one of you contains something special that you can contribute to the world. You're all talented, yes, but a talent is just something you're good at. You've got something even greater than a talent—you have a gift.

"Your gift is something that sums up the contribution of your life and encompasses your very essence. I want you all to find your gift and make it the core of your lives. Although your gift won't make you a million dollars, it will ensure that you are happy and that your life has meaning.

"Mushki, you possess a certain gentility. People confide in you and strangers turn to you, and that gives you an incredible power in social situations. You are a nurturer. If you foster that gift, you will bring healing to a great many broken souls.

"Chana, your gift is quite different. You are fire incarnate. You are excitement and dynamism personified, and people always love being around you because of your activity and your passion. Never allow it to diminish, and help set people's souls alight.

"Shterny, your gift has an artistic dimension. It's not about just being good with a paintbrush, a sketchbook, or a camera—it's more expansive than that. You see things other people don't see, perceive colors that are so delicate and subtle, and you have the ability to create the world anew through those perceptions.

"Mendy, your gift is the enlightenment that comes through knowledge and enlivening both yourself and others with the beauty and power of ideas. You have the gift of being able to rationally persuade people to see truths that would otherwise be obscured from them."

At the same time, I remind them, "Yet you all must understand that this is simply my understanding of your gifts. There is so much for you to figure out about yourselves, so much life ahead of you.

What I've told you is nothing but a hint, a clue, based on your father's incomplete perceptions.

"Above all, I want you to know that you *do* have gifts—amazing and unique gifts—and I want you to do precisely what you most want to, contributing to the world to the best of your ability. It's in your power to be just who you want to be. I am here to help you do just that."

You can help your children only so much. In the end, they need to live their own lives. Yet there is nothing more powerful than expressing your support for them in a serious conversation. It's the least that we, as parents, can do.

The scariest thing about finding your gift is the fact that once you've found it, you *don't* get a free ride for the rest of life. In fact, it's all too easy to forget your gift, given all of the distractions of the modern world. Time and again, I've nearly forgotten my own.

I have always considered myself fortunate to have known my gift from a relatively early age. God, in his infinite kindness, helped me discover my gift as a young man, even as it developed out of painful circumstances.

I'm a child of divorce. From the beginning, I knew that I would grow up to heal broken hearts and shattered families. That's what my own personal gift is: I am here to spread values. To remind all of us, myself included, of the things that are truly urgent and important in life.

I became a rabbi at Oxford when I was just twenty-two years old. My wife and I worked tirelessly to inspire students to embrace a spiritual life that was suffused with service to God and humanity. I taught, I wrote, and I organized huge speaker events and debates. My wife and I put on massive Friday night Sabbath dinners that demanded Herculean efforts. In the company of hundreds of students, we ate together, sang together, laughed together, and discussed the great issues of life as one.

As hard as it was, I couldn't have been happier. I was satisfied and deeply content to be using my gift to the fullest. I was inspiring young students, writing essays that thousands read each week, and changing people's lives. How could it get better than that?

But then, something shifted. My students, on whom I had waited hand and foot, graduated from Oxford and slowly began to emerge in their real-world careers. Some went on to make tens of millions of dollars on Wall Street, while others matured into famous, powerful politicians. As I watched their incredible successes, I began to question my own contribution. Compared to the people I had been preaching to for years, I felt small and insignificant. They had found a global stage. Mine was still confined to a university and its eighteen- to twenty-two-year-old students. My former students were making obscene amounts of money, while I struggled to make ends meet.

I had to ask myself, "*Am I a failure?* Perhaps my gift wasn't all that special to begin with. Maybe I could do what my students are doing. I could be a rabbi and maybe do business on the side. After all, I'm sick of not making enough to support, thank God, my large family.

"Or else I might run for office and change people's lives that way. I'm a good orator, and I have plenty of experience raising money. I'd have a much bigger platform if I did.

"Maybe I should just leave Oxford and find a respectable synagogue so that I can earn a regular salary. How long can I really go on running this student organization, relying primarily on book sales to support my family?"

What a mistake. I was ceasing to value *my* gift. I knew in my heart that I hadn't been placed on this earth to be another politician who is focused on power rather than values, or a conceited businessman. Many have followed that calling, but there's only one of me. And there were millions of broken hearts to be mended, millions of people looking for inspiration and direction. Given the level of need, why wasn't I valuing myself and my contribution? I then remembered a story I had heard in yeshiva when I was about eighteen years old.

There was once a rich man who invited poor people to his house on Friday nights. He took great pride in feeding the hungry. In the same town, there was a wagon driver who didn't make much money but who would drive people for whatever amount of money they had. If they had nothing, he'd take them anyway.

The rich man and the wagon driver saw each other at synagogue one day and struck up a conversation. The rich man said, "You know, I'm beginning to have doubts about my life. Am I really a good person? It's all too easy for me to have the cook make dinner and the servants clean up. I just pay for it to happen. That's not real charity. But what *you're* doing is amazing. You have to feed horses and keep them clean. You need to maintain your wagon. And still, you drive people to where they need to be for nothing. I wish I could do what you do."

The wagon driver responded, "What are you saying? What you're doing is really amazing! I help one or two people get where they need to go. But what if they didn't get there? They wouldn't die. But with you, if you don't feed them, they actually *will* die of hunger. I'm the one who deserves to question himself. I'm a nothing. A nobody. A real loser with nothing but my half-dead mule to offer."

The rich man and the wagon driver decided to switch places. The rich man became the wagon driver for a week, while the wagon driver stepped into the shoes of the rich man. He invited fifty people to his tiny, broken-down house for the Sabbath dinner. When they arrived, because this poor wagon driver had nothing to offer, there was only a small loaf of bread for the fifty people to share. They all left starving, having eaten no more than miniscule morsels of food. Meanwhile, the rich man found that he had no clue how to drive a wagon. He tried to saddle up the horses, but every time he jumped aboard he would just fall back into the mud. He was useless to everyone who needed to get somewhere.

Both men thought that the other had the more precious gift, but when they tried to switch, they each lost their way. They alone could perform the task they were doing.

The story sounds simple but contains enormous profundity for those of us searching for our innate gift.

In a capitalist society, we constantly compare ourselves with others. Yet although we can compete endlessly against one another for external advantage, we can never compete for an internal gift that is all our own. We each have something that makes us special and unique, and if we lose track of it along the way, we need to go back to the drawing board and find it all over again.

Speak to yourself. Find the voice of your deepest self, the most authentic part of your identity, and say with sincerity and resolve,

I've been thinking long and hard about what my unique contribution to the world is.

My gift is not the harsh words I sometimes utter to my kids in a fit of rage or the withering criticism I direct at my spouse in moments of great pressure. That is not the true me, and it is not my gift. It is someone else. It is the voice of someone mangled by the constant responsibilities of life.

Nor is my gift the money I make, the house I own, or the car I drive. I could live in a mud hut on the edge of town, and I would still be me—my possessions are inconsequential to my identity.

When I think about my gift, I remember a biblical story. Moses once said to God, "Teach me your glory, oh God. *Who are You, Lord?* You show Yourself in so many ways—Creator, Paternal Judge, Mother Nature. You make the sun shine and the rain fall. You raise the mountains to lofty peaks and carve out deep, luscious valleys. But behind all of that, Who are You?"

And from the darkness and the deep, God responded, "I am the Lord God, compassionate and gracious. Patient and long-suffering, and abundant in mercy and in truth. Granting mercy to thousands, forgiving sin and error and cleansing those in iniquity" (Exodus 34:6–7 NIV).

Incredible. God's very essence is compassion. God's being is mercy, kindness, and love. Created as I am in His image, *that is my essence as well.*

My gift is the love and kindness I practice with others. It is my capacity to listen to my friends when they are down. It is the kindness I show a stranger on the highway when he wants to cut in front of me. It is the little wave I give a child when I walk past her at the supermarket.

My gift is making others feel as if they matter.

My gift is calling my wife up during the day when I have nothing to tell her, other than that she is the kindest woman I know. My gift is making my children laugh at the dinner table with the silly imitations I do of their, and my, quirks and foibles.

My gift is curbing my anger at subordinates at work when they mess up. Instead, I call them into my office afterward and respectfully encourage them to do their best.

My gift is looking after my elderly parents with care and patience, just as they looked after me when I was a helpless child. My gift is sitting with the elderly and making them feel vibrant and appreciated. My gift is taking my kids for long bike rides and hikes so that they always know that my greatest joy is spending time with them.

My gift is patiently listening to my husband when he feels wounded. It is bolstering his ego when he feels down and telling him what a great man he is, even if he doesn't make a million dollars.

My gift is setting up single friends who are lonely and want to meet life partners.

My gift is keeping mum while my friends gossip about a colleague. Even better, it is when I politely, though never condescendingly, change the subject.

My gift is picking up pieces of trash that others threw on the sidewalk and keeping God's green earth beautiful.

My gift is being the first to greet all whom I meet and offering them a warm smile, regardless of how my day is going.

My gift is forgiving those who hurt me and trying to find mitigating circumstances behind their hurtful actions so that I never judge them too harshly.

My gift is saying a brief hello to strangers in an elevator, because no two human beings who ever meet are complete strangers.

All of these are but facets of my gift, my innate and unique contribution to the universe. I discover new sides to this contribution every day, and it is my heart's desire to continually learn more ways to express this goodness and thereby make my own righteous mark on the world.

Whenever I lose faith, feel downtrodden, or can't see my own value in the world, I will remember this. More than that, I will speak it aloud, honestly, and freely to myself in sustained conversation: *I will remember that there is no time I feel better than when I contribute my gift.*

To develop a personalized relationship with the voice of your innermost self, ask yourself the following questions. Respond to them, and let the answers guide you on self-talks of your own devising.

Am I at peace with who I am, or am I dissatisfied by my position in life?

Do I live with regret that I didn't become as successful as this or that friend?

Am I jealous of everyone around me? When I see a politician on TV, do I think I should have run for office? When I read about a billionaire philanthropist, do I kick myself for not being rich? If I'm watching sports, do I regret not becoming an athlete?

Do I always push my kids to embrace my path, rather than finding their own? Do I poke fun at my spouse's ambitions? Do I thereby snuff out his or her gift without noticing?

At the end of the day, have I allowed the voice of my innermost self to fall silent, or do I continue to remind myself of my particular gift and all that I, and only I, have to offer the world?

EPILOGUE

Who Do You Want to Be?

After I wrote the book *10 Conversations You Need to Have with Your Children*, one conversation most piqued readers' interest: when I told parents to ask their kids, "Who do you want to be?" That question is not among the ten conversations addressed explicitly in this book, but if you read closely, you'll see it touched on by every chapter in turn.

I often ask it of myself. "*Who is the man I want to be? What are his characteristics, and how does he act?*" It does me no good to be unrealistic—I'm only human, and I know my limitations. For that reason, when I look to history for instructive examples, more than most people, Thomas Jefferson speaks to me. He was a man whose life encompassed incredible contradictions. He gave eloquent voice to the desire for liberty, yet failed to free his own slaves. He vowed to fight oppression and defend liberty, yet almost certainly he had an intimate relationship with Sally Hemings, a black woman who may have had little to no choice in whether she desired this relationship.

Does that make him a hypocrite? A fraud? No. *It means he was human.* He succeeded spectacularly at some things and failed miserably at others. His eloquence in being America's most powerful voice on human liberty stemmed from what Abraham Lincoln would call "the better angels of our nature," while his indulgence in the abomination of slavery stemmed from the darker recesses of his soul. We all have selfish tendencies that defy our altruistic side, weaknesses along with our strengths, moments of bravery *and* cowardice. Thomas Jefferson experienced it all. This doesn't excuse the bad things he did. Nevertheless, as a man who struggled against his darker impulses and gave voice to the human spirit striving for liberty, Jefferson became the quintessential American character.

When I read biographies of Jefferson and histories of his era, I can't help but think, "That's partially me." I have experienced similar contradictions. There is no more deeply seated desire in my body than the desire to be righteous, just, and decent. Yet so many things get in the way. I want to be noble, I want to have a refined character, but it's a constant struggle to be selfless and to put others first. Life is a matter of always reminding myself who I want to be.

One night not too long ago my daughter went out with a young man. She came back from her date unable to stop smiling. As she shut the front door of the house, I went up to her and asked, "Did you like him?"

She said, "I really did. Do you remember all of those things you always say that a man should be? Someone who treats everyone with dignity and respect? Well, he was all of that and more: he was a gentleman."

That's precisely what I want to be. I want to be a gentleman. And the key to being that man is to speak to myself in a manner that encompasses all of the other conversations that have come before. That's right: it's time for me to have a self-talk of my own.

Just as you've been doing throughout this book, I sit myself down, shut my eyes, and attune myself to each frequency in turn: the inner voice of inspiration, of conscience, and of my innermost self. Once

I've drowned out the voices of the external world, it is time for me to ask myself:

How do I turn myself into the man I want to be? How can I make myself the gentleman it is within my reach to become? The answer is following my own advice—having these ten conversations with myself.

The first step is perfectly clear. Before I can do anything else, I must embrace hunger. I don't want to be stagnant. I don't want to grow complacent. I may be forty-four years old, but there's still plenty of fight in me. If there's any chance of stoking it, I need to feed off the undying desire for greater things that forever burns inside me.

Yet who am I? Living in the public eye is a part of my life, and I admit freely that attention gives me a certain satisfaction. A few years ago, I debated a renowned Christian scholar in New York City. I defended Judaism against the charge that it was an outdated religion, replaced by Christianity. The local Jewish community flocked to the debate to cheer me on. A friend of mine (who is himself a celebrity) watched the way people surrounded me when the debate was over, and he couldn't help but exclaim, "Hey, you're a rock star!" Okay, it felt good. Yet I know my life is about more than that. As great as the adulation feels, I yearn for the quieter, more fulfilling joys of life. I always want to try to act righteously, experience a sense of justice, and do right by my friends and family. That's why I need to choose love, not attention.

Yet at the same time, I don't want to go too far. I don't want to obliterate myself and my personal contribution by ignoring my ego. It's helped me do meaningful things. I've tried to stamp a distinctly Jewish, yet universal mark on the world, helping people heal their marriages and make their lives more purposeful, based on the Jewish values of respect, gratitude, and commitment. It's in no one's interests for me to repress my ambition and myself, because I know how important it is for me to give the ego its due.

Sometimes, despite my best intentions, I start to falter. I let myself get down, submitting to the death urge that is so prevalent in our culture. None of that is healthy. I have to defy and rise above such impulses.

Even more important, I have to remember to listen to my own advice. I tell couples all of the time that you shouldn't have a television in the bedroom. It ruins a couple's sex life, you don't read as much, and in general it keeps you and your spouse from connecting. Even so, when I started working on *Shalom in the Home*, I said to my wife, "Well, I've *got* to put a TV in the bedroom now. It's for work!" Soon enough, we were watching the news, documentaries. Yes, educational stuff, but it still pulls you away. I have nine kids, couples to counsel, books to write, lectures to give, and plenty of other things on my plate. I don't have any time to waste. That's why I've got to defy death.

Action is the most important thing, even when I don't feel inspired to act. Only when my goodness is anchored in real deeds do my intentions become solid. I therefore have to battle my instincts and resolve to do my way to feeling.

I must also be honest with myself. So often, I have done things that I thought were based on my value system, things that I thought would help me be a gentleman. Yet it turned out that my actions were motivated in part by the petty search for recognition. When I was working with Michael Jackson, I always had to ask myself, "Why am I Michael Jackson's rabbi?" Well, he was a good man with a deep desire to heal the world who had partially lost his way. That's true. Yet the outsized attention I received made me question my motives. In time I had to absent myself, once I realized I could no longer help him. Counseling celebrities leads to the same self-questioning, and that's exactly as it should be. I must always see myself in the third person. That's the only way I can ensure that I'm doing the right thing.

Being a blessing, not a burden, is what it's all about. I'll admit freely that I'm a damaged person. I'm all too susceptible to pressure and can be a burden to the people I love most. I need to remember that it's not just about me. My family has experienced enough pain through my parents' divorce. I need to be close to my siblings and their children and try to inspire while gaining inspiration from them. And let's not forget, of my nine children, five are in their teen years at the same time! They need my guidance. They can't have me coming through the door in a bad mood. I need to be there for them and be all the more of a blessing, so as to show them that life is a celebration and we dare not sweat the small stuff.

Embracing that blessing and fighting against being a burden will forever require me to struggle. My own struggles are so central to the person I want to be. I'm not looking to be perfect. In fact, I have no desire to be a perfectly monolithic saint. It would be inauthentic, even if it were possible to become so. My more difficult tendencies, my darker sides—they're just as much a part of me as my goodness is. Improving myself is not about destroying my contradictions; it's about thriving from the clash between them.

It's easy to become complacent. I'm a rabbi. I spent ten years studying Judaism. You'd think that I would know my way around the subject. But no, enlightenment is a never-ending process. There are always new texts, and the ones I've already studied demand constant reexamination. As Stephen Covey wrote in the *Seven Habits of Highly Effective People*, if you want to improve, you need to sharpen the saw. Our culture doesn't like to ask—it prefers easy answers. And it's all too easy to let yourself be dulled by the culture of celebrity that seems to reign over all. That's why I always have to sharpen my mind, increase my inquisitiveness, and always ask questions.

Despite everything, I sometimes feel as if I'm treading water. I get down and find it difficult to love myself. I need to know my gift, even when it's difficult. I have to stop looking at other people's gifts, defining myself by other people's examples. I have to stop looking at other people and being jealous of their scope or their talents. The only thing worthy of jealousy is being jealous of other people's virtue and seeking to emulate it, even as we find it in our own special way.

My gift is, first and foremost, to heal what was broken in my family. I have to be a good husband, be attentive to my wife, and give my children love, stability, and security. That's my gift: to be a good man, a good husband, and a gentleman. Not only that, but to model gentlemanliness for my sons and give my daughters an idea of the kind of men they ought to date. To give them enough love that they're never desperate for male attention.

I need to remember the big picture, too. I'm part of a people who have suffered character assassinations, expulsions, and holocausts. Part of my gift is giving honor to my people and dignity to Judaism.

Just the same, I am a member of the human family. I love the good-will that I can engender between people. I love the breadth of humanity that attends my Friday night Sabbath dinners—the Seventh-Day Adventists, Muslims, Mormons, atheists, blacks, whites, rich, poor, famous, and ordinary like me who all find common ground in simple conversation. I want to make my contribution to that unity.

My gift is to work toward enacting that ancient prophesy of Isaiah: "The wolf will live with the lamb, the leopard will lie down with the goat, the calf and the lion and the yearling together; and a little child will lead them. The cow will feed with the bear, their young will lie down together, and the lion will eat straw like the ox. The infant will play near the hole of the cobra, and the young child put his hand into the viper's nest. They will neither harm nor destroy on all my holy mountain, for the earth will be full of the knowledge of the LORD as the waters cover the sea" (Isaiah 11:6–9 NIV). Yes—this vision of peace energizes me every day.

I resolve to battle the predatory instincts in myself and the world at large. I will continue in my quest to be gentlemanly, and when I falter, as I inevitably will from time to time, I vow to engage myself in self-talks until I find my way back. That's how I can become the man I want to be.

The two people who brought me into this world and gave me life ultimately couldn't get along. Their parting brought darkness into my life, casting a long shadow over my happiness. Yet that experience has led me to seek new ways to bring people together. And by engaging the voice of my inner self in conversation, I will continue the never-ending task of making my gift real. That's my contribution: to improve myself, always be humble, counsel others, be a beacon of light that illuminates my own existence as well as that of those who cross my path, inspire my kids, heal broken hearts, mend troubled spirits, and keep my wife, God willing, smiling and happy.

Notes

Chapter 2: Choose Love, Not Attention

36   *Another survey reveals that a full fifth*   Peter Benson, *The Troubled Journey: A Portrait of 6th–12th Grade Youth* (Minneapolis: Search Institute, 1993).

Chapter 3: Give the Ego Its Due

56   *"A genuine relationship"*   Eckhart Tolle, *A New Earth: Awakening to Your Life's Purpose* (New York: Penguin, 2008), p. 84.

56   *"To create suffering without recognizing it"*   Ibid., p. 116.

56   *"the ego is in its essential nature"*   Ibid.

60   *The rabbis agreed merely*   Yet just before they were going to kill him, they realized the enormity of what was about to happen. "What should we do?" Talmud, Yoma 69B.

Chapter 9: Always Ask

172   *Fewer than 28 percent can name the chief justice of the Supreme Court*   "Well Known: Twitter; Little Known: John Roberts," Pew Research Center for the People and the Press, accessed August 31, 2010, http://people-press .org/report/635/; Cornelia Dean, "Scientific Savvy? In US, Not So Much," *New York Times*, August 30, 2005, accessed August 31, 2010, www.nytimes .com/2005/08/30/science/30profile.html?_r=1&ex=1125547200&en= 631977063d726261&ei=5070.

172   *While almost three-quarters of Americans recall that Freedom of Speech*   Freedom Project, www.freedomproject.us/files/pdf/survey_results_report_final.pdf.

172 *A full 26 percent of Americans aren't even aware that the United States* Marist Poll, http://maristpoll.marist.edu/72-don%E2%80%99t-know-much-about-history.

172 *Religion is also increasingly a mystery to us* Stephen Prothero, *Religious Literacy: What Every American Needs to Know—and Doesn't* (New York: HarperOne, 2007).

172 *In one recent study that asked American teenagers* Sam Dillon, "History Stumps U.S. Teens," *New York Times*, February 20, 2008, accessed August 31, 2010, www.nytimes.com/2008/02/26/education/27history.html; "2006 National Geographic-Roper Survey of Geographic Literacy," *National Geographic*, accessed September 21, 2010, www.nationalgeographic.com/roper2006/findings.html; Prothero.

174 *"I was on a long flight across the Pacific"* Bill Bryson, *A Short History of Nearly Everything* (New York: Broadway, 2003), 6.

186 *A poignant aphorism in the Talmud says* Talmud, Pirkei Avot 2:6.

Index